DI006588

The Multinational Corporation in the World Economy

Published for The Atlantic Institute, The Committee
for Atlantic Economic Cooperation, and The Atlantic
Council of the United States

PRAEGER SPECIAL STUDIES IN
INTERNATIONAL ECONOMICS AND DEVELOPMENT

The Multinational Corporation in the World Economy

DIRECT INVESTMENT IN PERSPECTIVE

Edited by

Sidney E. Rolfe
Walter Damm

Foreword by
David M. Kennedy

Introduction by
C. Douglas Dillon
Neil H. McElroy

PRAEGER PUBLISHERS
New York • Washington • London

UNIVERSITY OF VICTORIA
LIBRARY
Victoria, B. C.

The purpose of Praeger Special Studies is to make specialized research in U.S. and international economics and politics available to the academic, business, and government communities. For further information, write to the Special Projects Division, Praeger Publishers, Inc., 111 Fourth Avenue, New York, N.Y. 10003.

PRAEGER PUBLISHERS
111 Fourth Avenue, New York, N.Y. 10003, U.S.A.
5, Cromwell Place, London S.W.7, England

Published in the United States of America in 1970
by Praeger Publishers, Inc.

All rights reserved

© 1970 by Praeger Publishers, Inc.

Library of Congress Catalog Card Number: 73-98937

Printed in the United States of America

FOREWORD

David M. Kennedy
U.S. Secretary of the Treasury

This book is the result of an important and timely international conference sponsored by The Atlantic Council of the United States, The Committee for Atlantic Economic Cooperation, and The Atlantic Institute. Meeting in Washington, D.C., during May, 1969, the conference participants—primarily key business leaders from Europe, Japan, Canada and the United States—discussed a topic that is increasing daily in importance: the multinational corporation. The emergence of world-wide business organizations, their effect on world production, trade and international economic relations, and the advantages and problems associated with this commercial expansion were analyzed in depth during the three-day conference.

The significance of this international business development is great. The growth of output by multinational corporations is far outstripping even the very rapid increase in international trade among nations. In the process of multinational corporate growth, the developed economies of Europe, Japan, Canada and the United States are becoming increasingly interrelated and interdependent. Thus, in this sense, foreign direct investment is moving the nations of the world closer toward international economic integration.

The late nineteenth century saw the culmination of an historic transfusion of capital and labor from Europe to the developing United States. Coming primarily from the United Kingdom but also from Continental Europe, European investment capital was important in laying the foundation in the United States for the emergence of an advanced industrial society. I cannot help but speculate on the topics which participants in a similar conference 100 years ago might have discussed. Undoubtedly many of the issues discussed during the present conference would have been included at that time as well: the advantages of investing in a steadily expanding U.S. market, the effect of U.S. laws and regulations on the position of the foreign investor, and the impact of direct investment on international trade. The participants would, presumably, also have discussed the intensive development of the U.S. frontier which began in earnest following the Civil War, the inventiveness and competitiveness of U.S.

v

manufacturing firms, and the evident ability of these firms to develop and sell new products. Certainly, however, the Europeans at such a meeting would not have foreseen the emergence of the United States as the largest single market economy, outstripping even their own in size.

I believe that the future of the U.S. market is equally bright today as it was then. Farsighted investors of other nations will undoubtedly increase their participation in the future growth of the U.S. market, not only through trade but also through direct investments in the U.S. business community.

The papers presented at the May conference and now contained in this book appraise both the advantages and the problems facing foreign investors as they increase their direct investment stake in the U.S. economy. The ground rules for such investment are carefully restated and important topics requiring the added attention of government and business leaders everywhere are pointed out—the internationalization of production, the need for adequate public information on the operations of international corporations, the growth of international capital markets attuned to the needs of the multinational corporation, the relationship between the multinational corporation and the governments of countries in which it does business, and the need to maintain conditions which permit the free international flow of technology and capital.

David M. Kennedy

CONTENTS

Appendixes

LIST OF TABLES AND FIGURES

FIGURES

INTRODUCTION

C. Douglas Dillon and Neil H. McElroy

With few exceptions the participants of the conference, "Direct Investment in the Atlantic Area," were businessmen, leaders of their respective industries or financial institutions. As such they think of themselves as practical men. While they would not usually be considered visionary, certainly they are planners for the future, at least in the sense of thinking ahead about markets, investments, and business development. It is refreshing, indeed essential, that from time to time they take a fresh look at business—to see how their companies' actions fit into the broader scheme of economic relations in the world.

Even today's business leadership is a little awed by the enormous prosperity, the high standards of living, the huge volume of trade and investment that have developed in the postwar years, and particularly in more recent years during which many leaders have come to occupy their present positions. This development is the more remarkable since many clearly remember the struggles of the late 1940's and the real doubt that prevailed in many minds as to whether the private-enterprise system might give way, perhaps even to Communism, in the very heartland of our civilization, that is, in Western Europe. The fact that we are very much alive and well, and the fact of our great prosperity, are of course associated phenomena. Without vigorous private enterprise, we could not have had this prosperity. Those in business are in no small part responsible for the staggering economic success of the developed countries in the Atlantic Community and Japan—the areas with which we are primarily concerned in this book.

Political and military cooperation have also made essential contributions to the underlying stability without which there can be no economic progress. But even when, from time to time, political and military cooperation has been weakened by events, we have witnessed the continuing development of an economic structure based on mutual cooperation and mutual respect. And at heart that economic cooperation reflects the fact that business and banking leaders throughout the developed free world increasingly realize that they have, by and large, the same goals and needs.

Since the late 1940's, the economies of Western Europe and North America—and to an increasing extent Japan—have become indissolubly linked at an accelerating rate. This interdependence has been pioneered by private business, to its own profit, and to the benefit of the peoples of many lands. Conferences such as this help to develop a solid infrastructure of private-sector cooperation which both stimulates and facilitates constructive governmental action.

In 1965 and 1966, The Atlantic Institute and The Atlantic Council undertook a series of general economic meetings, bringing together businessmen from several countries, in Paris, Fontainebleau, Crotonville, New York, and Geneva, to discuss matters of mutual interest.

From the Geneva meeting there came a recommendation that a committee be formed to continue to undertake such meetings and to focus them on timely problems which could be examined in some depth. These deliberations were to be more than academic: Recommendations were to be drawn and pressed through whatever channels, governmental or other, were deemed appropriate. The desire to establish such a committee, devoted equally to thought and action, reflects the growing recognition—earlier alluded to—of our common needs and our capacity for effective international cooperation.

The Committee for Atlantic Economic Cooperation (CAEC) was the vehicle which grew out of the Geneva recommendation. In 1969, this committee, of which Aurelio Peccei has served as Chairman, included, in addition, Lord Sherfield from the United Kingdom, André Danzin from France, Robert Fowler from Canada, Wilfrid Guth from Germany, Johan Melander from Norway, Gerrit van der Wal from the Netherlands, and the authors of this Introduction from the United States. The Director General of The Atlantic Institute in Paris serves as an ex officio member, and Sidney Rolfe acts as Executive Secretary and as Director of Conferences.

In conjunction with the Business and Industry Advisory Council to the Organization for Economic Co-operation and Development (OECD) and with The Atlantic Institute, the CAEC undertook the Cannes Conference in 1967 on "Capital Markets"; with The Institute, the Rome Conference in 1968 on "Strategies for Atlantic Technological Development"; and in 1969, with The Institute and The Atlantic Council, the conference on "Direct Investment in the Atlantic Area." From past meetings, there emerged remarkably unified ideas and calls to action. Men long on talent and short of time used their time not only to attend these conferences but to work to implement their findings as well. The list of past chairmen of these conferences is a distinguished one: Dr. Herman Abs, Paul-Henri Spaak, Lauris Norstad, Wilfrid Baumgartner, and David Rockefeller are among them.

These meetings served to increase an understanding in depth of the issues to which they were addressed. Because of these meetings, many leaders now know one another better; they have defined and expressed common views and desires more clearly, and their respective views, more in harmony than in discord, have been listened to by their respective governments. Hopefully, and this is largely on agenda for the future, they will be able better to press their views and see them become policy.

The Committee for Atlantic Economic Cooperation launched plans for the conference, "Direct Investment in the Atlantic Area," in November, 1968, after the U.S. elections were held. They were then impressed that a significant political changing of the guard had taken place in the United States. Consequently, it was appropriate that business leaders of the developed world should meet the new Administration, and, equally important, the Administration should meet them.

Obviously, no one could have then foreseen the dramatic coincidence of this meeting and the turn of events in France in 1969. What the consequences of General Charles de Gaulle's departure would be, no man could then say. But Europe is not likely to be the same.

This is said in no sense antipathetically to the General or to France. On the contrary, but both in the United States and France these events reinforce the changing nature of political establishments, in contrast to the continuing and largely similar needs of the business sector of all countries. Political establishments make policies, and those policies can determine the fate of the economic community. It is therefore crucial that all leaders offer their best advice in helping to shape that fate.

Thus the conference and this volume are a logical development from the past, and it is hoped that this will not be the end of the road. The subject to which this book addresses our attention, "Direct Investment in the Atlantic Area," is both compelling and broad. There is reason to believe that at this time a special focus of attention should be on the expansion of direct investment by the major European companies in the United States. We all appreciate the difficulties implicit in this idea. But we wonder if those difficulties might not in the past have been exaggerated, whether in this regard our European counterparts are not victims of the focus on problems which exclude from their vision an equal focus on the opportunities in the United States. The United States is also aware that it would benefit from the contributions which Europe can make to its economic development through technical and other skills. We might also derive a short-run advantage to the U.S. balance of payments from such investment. But we all know that these investments are not short-run affairs; they last a long time and the full benefit of them to both parties comes only after nurturing and seasoning. The advantages from the European side are also very great. Many of them are spelled out in this volume.

Many of us on both sides of the Atlantic have acquired a deep, vested interest in each other's economies. These are the sinews of our common interests. In times past, the European interest in the economy of North America has greatly exceeded American interest in Europe. Recently, the pendulum has swung rapidly in the other direction. We will all be better off and future growth will be welcomed more wholeheartedly if a better balance can be achieved.

This conference was structured to provide one session on the international corporation in perspective, one on the Canadian and European experience with U.S. direct investment, one on external direct investment in the United States, one to provide a frank and off-the-record discussion between the private sector and key representatives of the new U.S. Administration, and a final session to formulate specific recommendations to both governments and business.

It would be remiss not to take this occasion to thank those men who have prepared the thoughtful background which went into this volume: Walter Damm, J. J. A. Ellis, Rainer Hellmann, Thomas L. Powrie, and Sidney E. Rolfe, and to extend our thanks as well to Wilfrid Guth, G. Arnold Hart, and C. F. Karsten, who chaired three of the working sessions of the conference.

A NOTE ON ORGANIZATION OF THE VOLUME

Sidney E. Rolfe

This volume, in its organization, regroups the ideas of the conference. Consequently, a word about organization might serve as a guide through the book.

The major quest of the conference was to examine the state of direct international investment, i.e., investment by corporations in production and distribution facilities in countries other than their own, and to make recommendations. A major emphasis within this general question fell on ways to increase direct investment by European and Japanese corporations into the United States. The prospect of increased foreign investment in the United States has been lauded by U.S. Government officials as an appropriate way to assist the U.S. balance of payments. Economists, who believe that a significant danger to the multinational corporation (and hence to the process of direct international investment), is the myth that the multinational corporation is overwhelmingly American-born and part of "the American invasion" of other lands also favor increased investment in the United States. It is true that this myth can be largely dispelled even now by a realistic look at existing statistics; but statistics are rarely widely read, so countervailing "invasions" of the U.S. market by foreign direct investment—of which there were some $9 billion in 1968—may lead to more effective demything.

The first part of this volume may be termed broadly introductory, designed to provide a perspective of the nature of foreign investment in general. In this category falls the Introduction by former Secretaries C. Douglas Dillon and Neil H. McElroy. Dr. Rolfe's "perspective view," in Chapter 2, which attempts to provide both statistical and qualitative analysis about the present and the visible future of the international corporation, also fits here.

Obviously of key importance, if European direct investment into the United States is to grow, are the European attitudes toward it. And the European views comprise Chapters 2 and 3. In Chapter 2, Dr. Walter Damm examines, largely from an economic point of view, the problems to be encountered and the attitudes of companies that have taken the plunge into the vast and competitive American market. In Chapter 3, Dr. J. J. A. Ellis looks at much the same problem from the legal point of view, and concludes that the American antitrust laws constitute a significant barrier to European investment in the United States. This is so not only because the Europeans are not as used to dealing with laws vigorously enforcing competition as are their American business counterparts, but also because American antitrust officials have extended the purview of their jurisdiction beyond the national border. Consequently, Ellis warns that European companies producing in the United States, although they are not American nationals, may find themselves subject, even abroad, to these American antitrust laws.

Chapter 4 consists of an American legal reply to Dr. Ellis's thesis by the Honorable Richard W. McLaren, Assistant Attorney General. Mr. McLaren contends that the United States welcomes European companies, but they must abide by the standards of American law applied to all here; that the very rules of competition being assailed make it possible for Europeans to want to invest in the U.S.; and, finally, that most potential extraterritorial applications of American antitrust law never, in fact, happen.

The review of attitudes of Europeans toward American investment in Europe is a well-ploughed field but one which merits continuing attention. Dr. Rainer Hellmann analyzes this question from a current perspective in Chapter 5. He notes, among other trends, that Europeans continue to invite American investment, even when many Americans borrow capital in Europe for such investment, because investment brings with it the transfer of up-to-date technology, a prime desire of European governments.

Then, in Chapter 6, Dr. Thomas L. Powrie examines the special problems of Canada. While its industries are largely foreign and usually U.S.-owned (which grates on nationalistic sentiments), Canada has one of the world's highest living standards, as a result. Canada thus faces the trade-off between economic benefits and political costs—a problem not unknown in other countries—in magnified form.

In Chapter 7, the conference recommendations and summary are presented verbatim. It is noteworthy that the conferees opted heavily in favor of continued free international investment with a minimum of government restriction and made some specific recommendations for the modification of U.S. antitrust procedures.

Finally, the volume includes, as Appendix A, a background paper prepared for the conference by the U.S. Department of Commerce, which is rich in statistical information. Appendix B, also by the Department of Commerce, lists foreign firms operating in the United States.

LIST OF PARTICIPANTS AT THE CONFERENCE, "DIRECT INVESTMENT IN THE ATLANTIC AREA"

Participants from the Private Sector

Belgium

Mr. Charles Desclée de Maredsous
Administrateur de Electrobel, E.B.E.S.,
Intercom et Compagnie Occidentale de
    Participations et de Gestion

Mr. Marc Verhaeghe de Naeyer
Président
Tréfileries Leon Bekaert S.P.R.L.

Prof. Dr. Luc Wauters
Vice Président du Conseil d'Administration
    et Président du Comité de Direction
Kredietbank S.A.
    (Member, Conference Steering Committee)

Canada

Hon. J. V. Clyne
Chairman of the Board
MacMillan, Bloedel, Ltd.

Mr. Marcel Faribault
Former President
General Trust Company of Canada

Mr. G. Arnold Hart
Chairman and President
Bank of Montreal
    (Chairman, Conference Working Session
    No. 2)

Mr. W. Earle McLaughlin
Chairman and President
Royal Bank of Canada

France

Mr. André Bouillot
Vice-Président Directeur Général de la
    Société Nationale des Pétroles d'Aquitaine
    (SNPA)

Mr. André Danzin
Vice-Président Directeur Général
THOMSON-CSF
    (Member, Committee for Atlantic Economic
    Cooperation and also Conference Steering
    Committee)

Mr. Robert Lattes
Directeur Général Adjoint du Groupe SEMA
    (Société d'Economie et de Mathématique Appliquée)

Mr. Noël Pouderoux
Président Directeur Délégué
Commission Générale d'Organisations Scien-
    tifiques (CEGOS)

Mr. Maurice Schlogel
Directeur Général
Crédit Lyonnais

Germany

Dr. Wilfrid Guth
Managing Director
Deutsche Bank A.G.
    (Member, Committee for Atlantic Economic
    Cooperation and also Conference Steering
    Committee; Chairman, Conference Work-
    ing Session No. 1)

Dr. Kurt Lotz
Chairman of the Managing Board
Volkswagenwerk A.G.

Mr. Alwin Münchmeyer
President Bundesverband deutscher Banken e.V.
Partner Schröder, Munchmeyer, Hengst & Co.

Mr. Wolfgang Reuter
Chairman of the Managing Board
DEMAG A.G.

Dr. Dieter Spethmann
Chairman of the Managing Board
Deutsche Edelstahlwerke A.G.
    (Member, Conference Steering Committee)

Dr. Gerd Tacke
Chairman of the Managing Board
Siemens A.G.

Italy

Dr. Franco Bobba
General Manager
Istituto Finanziario Industriale

Dr. Carlo Bombieri
Managing Director
Banca Commerciale Italiana

Professor Alberto Ferrari
Managing Director
Banca Nazionale del Lavoro

Professor Ernesto Manuelli
President
Societa Finanziaria Siderurgica

Dr. Franco Mattei
Deputy Secretary General
Confederazione Generale dell'Industria
    Italiana

Dr. Aurelio Peccei
Amministratore Delegato
Italconsult
    (Chairman, Committee for Atlantic Economic
    Cooperation; Member, Conference Steering
    Committee)

Japan

Mr. Norishige Hasegawa
President
Sumitomo Chemical Company

Mr. Yasushi Kaneko
Representing
The Mitsui Bank, Ltd.

Mr. Masao Kanno
Vice Chairman and Secretary General
Japanese BIAC to the OECD

Netherlands

Mr. L. E. J. Brouwer
President
Royal Dutch Shell

Dr. C. F. Karsten
Managing Director
Amsterdam-Rotterdam Bank N.V.

Prof. Dr. P. Kuin
Director
Unilever N.V. & Ltd.

Mr. John H. Loudon
Chairman of the Board
Royal Dutch Petroleum Company
    (Chairman of the Board, The Atlantic
    Institute)

Dr. G. van der Wal
President
KLM Royal Dutch Airlines
    (Member, Committee for Atlantic Economic
    Cooperation and also Conference Steering
    Committee)

Norway

Mr. Johan Holte
Director General
Norsk Hydro Elektrisk

Mr. Johan Melander
Managing Director
Den Norske Creditbank
    (Member, Committee for Atlantic Economic
    Cooperation and also Conference Steering
    Committee)

Sweden

Mr. Rune Hoeglund
Managing Director
Svenska Handelsbanken

Mr. Curt R. Nicolin
Director General
Almanna Svenska Elektriska A/B

Mr. Marc Wallenberg, Jr.
President
Stockholms Enskilda Bank
    (Member, Conference Steering Committee)

Switzerland

Dr. Edgar F. Paltzer
General Manager
Swiss Bank Corporation

Dr. Dr. h. c. Victor H. Umbricht
Managing Director
CIBA Limited

United Kingdom

Lord Aldington, P.C., K.C.M.G., C.B.E., D.S.O., T.D.
Chairman
National & Grindlays Bank

Sir Frank Kearton
Chairman
Courtaulds Limited

Mr. J. Martin Ritchie
Chairman
Bowater Paper Corporation

Sir Eric Roll, K.C.M.G., C.B.
S. G. Warburg & Co., Limited

Lord Sherfield, G.C.B., G.C.M.G.
Chairman
Hill, Samuel & Co., Limited
    (Member, Committee for Atlantic Economic
    Cooperation and also Conference Steering
    Committee)

United States

Mr. James H. Binger
Chairman
Honeywell Incorporated

Mr. Fred J. Borch
Chairman
General Electric

Hon. W. Michael Blumenthal
President
Bendix International

Hon. Frederick L. Deming
Partner
Lazard Freres

Mr. Russell De Young
Chairman
Goodyear Tire & Rubber Company

Hon. C. Douglas Dillon
President
United States and Foreign Securities
    Corporation
    (Member, Committee for Atlantic Economic
    Cooperation and also Conference Steering
    Committee)

Hon. Henry H. Fowler
Goldman, Sachs & Co.

Hon. Thomas S. Gates
Chairman of the Executive Committee
Morgan Guaranty Trust Company

Mr. Robert L. Genillard
General Partner
White, Weld & Co.

Mr. Yves-André Istel
Partner
Kuhn, Loeb & Co.

Hon. Neil H. McElroy
Chairman of the Board
The Procter & Gamble Company
    (Chairman of the Conference; Member,
    Committee for Atlantic Economic
    Cooperation and also Conference Steering
    Committee)

Mr. Herbert P. Patterson
President
Chase Manhattan Bank

Mr. J. Howard Rambin, Jr.
Chairman of the Board
Texaco Incorporated

Mr. George Russell
Vice Chairman
General Motors Corporation

Mr. Charles H. Sommer, Jr.
Chairman
Monsanto Chemical Company

International Organizations

Mr. Frederic Boyer de la Giroday
Director for Monetary Matters
Directorate General for Economic and
    Financial Affairs
European Economic Communities

Hon. Walter Dowling
Director General
The Atlantic Institute
    (Member, Committee for Atlantic Economic
    Cooperation and also Conference Steering
    Committee)

Mr. Emile van Lennep
Secretary General Elect
Organization for Economic Cooperation and
    Development

Mr. A. F. K. Schlepegrell
Head of Current Invisibles and Capital
    Markets Division
Organization for Economic Cooperation and
    Development

Authors of Conference Working Papers

Dr. Thomas L. Powrie
Associate Director of Research
Canadian Trade Committee
Private Planning Association of Canada

Dr. Rainer Hellmann
Brussels Bureau Chief
Vereinigte Wirtschaftsdienste GmbH

Dr. Walter Damn
Secretary
Fédération Bancaire de la C.E.E.

Dr. J. J. A. Ellis
Advocaat en Procureur
The Hague

Conference Director

Dr. Sidney E. Rolfe
Executive Secretary
Committee for Atlantic Economic
    Cooperation

Deputy Conference Director

Mr. Joseph W. Harned
Assistant Director
The Atlantic Council of the United States

**Officials of The Atlantic Council of the
    United States**

Hon. W. Randolph Burgess
Chairman, Executive Committee

Hon. Theodore C. Achilles
Vice Chairman, Executive Committee

Mr. Richard J. Wallace
Director General

Mr. Gene Bradley
Member, Board of Directors

Hon. Samuel C. Waugh
Member, Board of Directors

Observers

Mr. Johnson Garrett
Industrial Development Attaché for Europe

Mr. Henry Koch
Manager, Participations and Portfolio Sales
International Bank for Reconstruction and
  Development

Dr. Kazuo Nukazawa
United States–Japan Trade Council

United States Government Officials

Hon. William P. Rogers
Secretary of State

Hon. Maurice Stans
Secretary of Commerce

Hon. David M. Kennedy
Secretary of the Treasury

Dr. Arthur F. Burns
Counsellor to the President
The White House

Hon. Paul Volcker
Under Secretary of the Treasury for Monetary
  Affairs

Dr. Paul W. McCracken
Chairman
Council of Economic Advisors

Hon. Paul Rand Dixon
Chairman
Federal Trade Commission

Hon. Andrew F. Brimmer
Governor
Federal Reserve System

Hon. Richard B. Smith
Commissioner
Securities and Exchange Commission

Nathaniel Samuels
Deputy Under Secretary of State for
    Economic Affairs
    (Session Chairman)

Hon. Edwin Cohen
Assistant Secretary of the Treasury for Tax
    Policy

Hon. Richard W. McLaren
Assistant Attorney General

Hon. Kenneth Davis
Assistant Secretary of Commerce for Domestic
    and International Business

Mr. Lawrence A. Fox
Director
Bureau of International Commerce
Department of Commerce

Mr. S. Stanley Katz
Director
Office of International Investment
Department of Commerce

Mr. Johnson Garrett
U.S. Industrial Development Attaché for
    Europe
Office of International Investment
Department of Commerce

Mr. Wilbur H. Fugate
Chief, Foreign Commerce Section
Anti-Trust Division
Department of Justice

The Multinational Corporation in the World Economy

1

THE INTERNATIONAL CORPORATION IN PERSPECTIVE

Sidney E. Rolfe

INTRODUCTION

The instrument which carries on direct investment, which has made it a major force in the world economy, and which will determine its future, is the international corporation. The task at hand is to provide a perspective view of the direct-investment phenomenon. To do so, four deceptively simple questions suggest themselves. First, where do we stand today? A brief if so-called revisionist look at the statistics and new trends in international direct investment should create a quantitative frame of reference. Second, how did we get there? A very brief look at some past developments might enable us to avoid remaking past mistakes, or at any rate, to recognize them when made. Third, what are the consequences of the international corporation's efforts? A vast process of economic integration seems under way in the developed world, which is of great economic benefit, but which raises new questions as it solves old ones. And finally, some interpretation is required of the national response patterns, covered in detail in other chapters. All opinions expressed are, of course, the responsibility of the author.

A perspective view is being sought not only at the meeting from which this volume arose but in the numerous university, research, governmental, and other inquires now under way. It is essential that businessmen should give at least as much thought to this question as other establishments do. For a perspective view is most comparable to the religious notion of eschatology, that vision of the future which gives the present motive. Perspectives or eschatologies have a way of becoming self-fulfilling prophecies.

A new world economy is taking shape, largely as a result of the internationalization of production—or as one French writer has phrased it, "planetisation." Its ultimate shape is yet unknown. It is in evolution, and its ultimate shape will be molded by the policies of government, business, and

5

others. And that shape will in turn depend on the vigor and persuasiveness of those now seeking perspectives. International business can help shape the future: If it remains passive and provincial in its view, it will simply be shaped by the vision of others, perhaps less qualified.

WHERE WE STAND: PATTERNS AND TRENDS

Judd Polk first pointed out that the value of production abroad of American-owned international subsidiaries appeared to be twice the value of American direct investment abroad.[1] This 2:1 ratio is a rule-of-thumb estimate but probably a pretty good one. Based on 1967 data, output in the vicinity of $120 billion per annum resulted from U.S. direct investment of some $60 billion. This output, Polk noted, was more than the Gross National Product (GNP) of any free nation outside the United States. Further, Polk pointed out that the rate of growth of international production exceeded the growth rate of most nations, and, by considerable bounds, the rate of growth of exports; U.S. exports of $30 billion in that year were indeed dwarfed by the output figure. Polk went further and added that the total value of production abroad of U.S.-owned assets was more like $180 billion, if the output of companies in which U.S. companies owned shares was added to the direct-investment total.

Some scholars have since caviled at the rule-of-thumb ratios which Polk employed. But no one has questioned the inference from his data: That, at least in the case of the United States, international investment had bypassed exports as the main channel of international economic relations. This observation is underscored when it is recognized that a full 25 per cent of all U.S. exports are shipped within or to subsidiaries of U.S.-owned international corporations. A startling and to some eyes new phenomenon had suddenly appeared on the economic horizon.

Polk's datum, or at any rate a close facsimile of it, became a key weapon in the hands of Servan-Schreiber whose *Le Defi Americain* announced to millions of readers that the third-largest producing unit in the world after the United States and the U.S.S.R. was the economy of American subsidiaries abroad. Clearly a phenomenon so startling and so broad deserves a closer look.

And, on further examination, new, severely modifying, and key conclusions have emerged. The first is that *le defi* is not in fact American but rather international. Part of the focus on U.S. investments stems from fear of the very size of U.S. corporations; more objectively, it is obvious that U.S.-based corporations have dominated the international investment scene in the 1958-68

---

[1] Judd Polk, "The New World Economy," *Columbia Journal of World Business* (January–February, 1968).

decade. The OECD, in assembling data for other nations as well as the United States—a process that involved not only the examination of official sources which are very often wholly unrevealing but also company balance sheets, assorted balance-of-payments flows data, some direct samplings, and some estimates—emerged in 1968 with a set of data relating to 1966 which put a surprisingly different face on the matter. The direct investment assets abroad owned by companies of countries other than the United States totaled some $35 billion, compared to $55 billion for the United States, and these are roughly comparable to the Gross National Products of the countries involved.

These data are presented more fully in Tables 1 and 2. A cursory glance, particularly at Table 2, will show the rudimentary nature of available international comparative information on direct investment, even when the OECD estimates, the best available, are used. It is perhaps significant that for the Netherlands and Switzerland, the countries whose foreign direct investment is thought to be a larger per cent of their GNP than any other countries, data are so lacking that they car. only be included in totals, without any breakdown.

TABLE 1

**Estimated Accumulated Overseas Direct Investments
of DAC Countries, End 1966
(millions of dollars)**

	World Total	Less-Developed Countries Total	Less-Developed Countries Percentage of Total
Petroleum	25,942	11,892	46
Mining and Smelting	5,923	2,801	47
Manufacturing	36,246	8,047	22
Other	21,472	7,230	33
Total	89,583	29,970	33

Note: Development Assistance Committee (DAC) countries include: Belgium, Canada, France, Germany, Italy, Japan, Netherlands, Sweden, Switzerland, United States, and United Kingdom.

Source: OECD, DAC (68) 14, 23 April, 1968, p. 28.

TABLE 2

Direct Foreign Investment, Accumulated Assets, by Major Countries, End 1966
(book value, in millions of dollars)

	World	U.S.	U.K.	France	Germany	Sweden	Canada	Japan
Petroleum	25,942	16,264	4,200	d	200	a	a	a
(LDC)	(11,892)	(6,975)	(2,167)	(670)	(65)	a	a	(222)
Mining and Smelting	5,923	4,135	759	a	100	a	250[b]	a
(LDC)	(2,801)	(1,827)	(298)	(200)[b]	(38)	(65)	(202)	(71)
Manufacuring	36,246	22,050	6,028	a	1,800	a	2,988[b]	a
(LDC)	(8,047)	(4,124)	(1,471)	(1,230)[b]	(645)	(96)	(332)	(270)
Other	21,472	12,113	5,015[c]	a	400	a	a	a
(LDC)	(7,230)	(3,915)	(2,255)	a	(97)	a	a	(33)
Total	89,583	54,462	16,002	4,000[b]	2,500	793	3,238	1,000
(LDC)	(29,970)	(16,841)	(6,184)	(2,100)	(845)	(161)	(534)	(605)

Note: Italy, Holland, Switzerland, and Belgium data not available; Australia total investment is $300 million.

[a] Not available.

[b] Estimate.

[c] Including agriculture of 1,022 (864 in the less-developed countries, or LDC's).

[d] Total French oil production estimated at 57.2 million tons in 1966.

Source: Compiled from OECD, DAC (68) 14, Annex C (April 23, 1968).

When the Polk projection on the 1966 OECD data is used, it follows that the world output from foreign-owned subsidiaries of international corporations lies somewhere between $180 and $270 billion per annum; by some statistical juggling, the tentative figure of $240 billion may be appropriate. In comparison, exports from the major nations of the world totaled some $130 billion in 1967. It is therefore clear that for the whole developed world, international investment has bypassed exports as the major channel of international economic relations. It is also apparent that direct investment is a far more balanced phenomenon than had been thought.

It also follows that a good part of *le defi americain* lies in *les statistiques americaines*. For the very availability of good U.S. data has in the past created a lopsided picture of world developments which tends to exacerbate the nationalist apprehensions about U.S. gigantism. Unfortunately, writers in every land find the use of U.S. data the path of least resistance in their task and tend to focus the problem where only part of it lives. If reasoned policy judgments are to be made in future, better data are critically needed.

Even a general awareness that direct investment, considered regionally, is in rough conformity to GNP will not dispel all of the fears about U.S. gigantism. For each individual nation may see its total only versus the United States, each a David facing the same Goliath. This perception could change rapidly if transnational mergers in Europe were to transpire; but the legal, fiscal, and psychological barriers to such mergers still stand, although under attack.

A complete picture, over time, is not available for all countries on the type and locale of international direct investment. But U.S. data, detailed in Table 3, seem to be indicative of world trends. These suggest a massive shift from the original international extractive industry investments to manufacturing and "other" (trade, banking, services, etc.), as well as a further shift from developing to developed countries. International investment is thus largely an interpenetration of the advanced economies by other advanced economies, for manufacturing.

There are yet other balancing statistics in this interregional comparison to which allusion may be made. This first lies in trends. Stated briefly, there is strong indication that U.S. investment, particularly in Europe, is now tending to taper off, not as a result of the capital controls but rather because of overcapacity. This trend was forecast in 1968 by a McGraw-Hill study, detailed in Figure 1. The Chase Manhattan Bank's *International Finance* corroborates the forecast, pointing to a 10 per cent decline in U.S. investment in Western Europe in 1968, owing largely to overcapacity.[2]

At the same time, the available data show a remarkable increase in direct investment from Continental Europe. Between 1962 aand 1967, France

---

[2]Chase Manhattan Bank, *International Finance*, April 14, 1969.

TABLE 3

Growth of United States Direct Investments, 1929-66
(billions of dollars = $000 million)

	1929	1946	1957	1966
Total	7.5	7.2	25.2	54.6
Areas				
Canada	2.0	2.5	8.6	16.8
Europe[a]	1.4	1.0	4.1	16.2
Latin America	3.5	3.1	8.4	9.9
Middle East and Africa[a]	0.1	0.2	1.8	3.7
Other Areas[a]	0.5	0.4	2.6	7.9
Industries				
Manufacturing	1.8	2.4	8.0	22.1
Petroleum	1.1	1.4	9.0	16.3
Mining and Smelting	1.2	0.8	2.4	4.1
Public Utilities	1.6	1.3	2.1	2.3
Other Industries	1.8	1.3	3.7	9.8

[a]Including developed and less-developed countries together.

Sources: 1926-57, "U.S. Business Investments in Foreign Countries," U.S. Department of Commerce, 1960; 1966, *Survey of Current Business* (September, 1967).

FIGURE 1

Forecast of U.S. Direct Investment Abroad to 1970

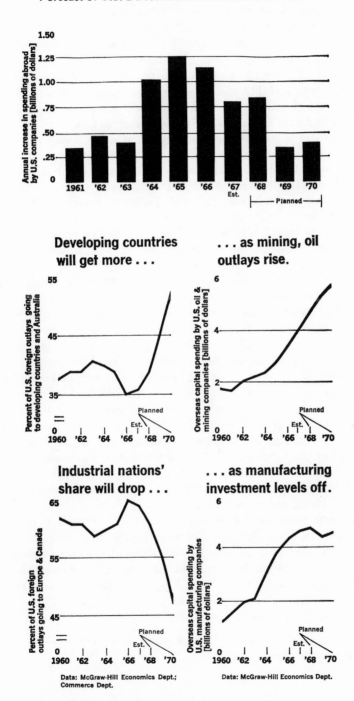

Source: *Business Week*, August 3, 1968.

increased her direct investment some 300 per cent; by the end of that span, France was investing about as much abroad as others were investing in France. And these data exclude the old French Empire, doubtless the recipient of much French investment, because until 1967 this was included in Metropolitan France for accounting purposes. Germany, by Bundesbank reckoning, increased its direct investment from DM 3.8 billion in 1961 to over DM 12 billion in 1967. While these data probably understate the true totals, this is a trend likely to advance in the future. The recent Swedish experiences are not dissimilar; Harald Lund's report for the Federation of Swedish Industries tells the story.[3]

It is of course too early to assess these trends. But it may well be that in retrospect the rush of U.S. investments from 1958-68 will appear a one-time move to match U.S.-based investment to its GNP capability and that in future the rate of new U.S. investment will slow as European-based foreign investment advances. Among the factors inducing foreign investment, technological or managerial "leads" are essential. The fact is that technology and corporate organization in all of the advanced countries have now reached levels of capability that permit focus on markets and production across, and indeed without reference to, national boundaries.

The 1970's are therefore apt to be characterized by rapidly increasing European direct investments. In the past, this has been directed largely to other European or to developing economies. One of the questions with which this volume deals is that of increased European direct investment to the United States. In Chapter 2 Dr. Damm covers the pros and cons of this matter, but perhaps a few observations may be underscored or stated here.

Dr. Damm's observation that the "decision is up to management" suggests that technological and managerial advantages exist on both sides of the Atlantic. Consequently, the former fear of many European managers that their techniques are inadequate is no longer true. His observation that the American market consists in fact of a number of submarkets suggests that the investment need not be gargantuan at the outset, i.e., that the whole American market need not be tackled at once. This observation is underscored by the fact that Europeans have some $7 billion successfully invested in the United States; as Appendix B shows, much of it is from smaller companies.

But these observations may be extended. The U.S. market, evidenced by GNP, represents about half the free world's total. It is difficult to see how international investment can proceed very far until this vast potential is fully exploited by foreign investors. And the fact that U.S. techniques are in many areas more advanced that European techniques constitutes a reason to invest in the United States as much as a deterrent.

---

[3]Harald Lund, *Swedish Business Abroad 1960-65* (Stockholm: Federation of Swedish Industries, December, 1964).

The benefits of investment, from the investor's point of view, are often thought to be limited to profitable operation. However, another dimension of benefit might be called the technical feedback of knowledge. Basically there are two ways in which such a feedback can result to the investing company. First, there is the access to knowledge of new products, technological materials, and managerial methods which would not otherwise be obtained; and second, there is the need to be more efficient, derived either from operating in a more competitive economic environment or from facing a factor-price structure, e.g., higher wage rates, conducive to a better deployment of resources.

In an analysis of British investment in the United States, J. Dunning concludes, from the British point of view, that

> such gains may well prove important when an investment is made in technologically advanced areas, e.g., North America. ... Thus, some 82.8 per cent of firms with manufacturing subsidiaries in the U.S. ... claimed they had derived some benefit in the form of technological knowledge and the exchange of ideas as a direct result of their investment ...

> [The] competitive stimulus forces the companies to adopt the most efficient production techniques and ... the knowledge so gained can often be successfully applied in the U.K. This sort of gain was very apparent in the case of firms which had a near monopoly or safe market position in the U.K., but had to fight for their existence in the foreign market.[4]

Professor Dunning also cites the positive advantages of investment in high wage areas:

> the impetus to mechanize is greater in the U.S. and Canada due to the higher price of labor and more extensive markets, but it is also true that the production methods so induced can often be applied with profit in the U.K. ... this was observed by a number of firms with investment interests in North America, e.g., by those in the chemical and textile industries. Clearly, this particular feedback effect does not apply to the same extent in the low wage areas.[5]

---

[4] J. Dunning, "Does Foreign Investment Pay?" *Moorgate and Wall Street* (Autumn, 1964).

[5] *Ibid.*

Dunning concedes that the value of this technical transference cannot be quantified. But he argues that it is a factor which must be taken into account when the private and social justification for investment overseas is considered. That is, even if there is some private trepidation at entering competitive markets, the social benefit to the investing country is very great when investment is made in a country which (1) has a more competitive environment, and (2) is industrially more advanced than the investing country.

Although Dunning analyzed this experience in the case of British firms, it has been reported by other firms as well. Olivetti, for example, indicates that one of the major advantages of its U.S. investment has been the improvement of techniques throughout the corporation.

Yet another element which would seem to facilitate increased European investment in the United States is the greater availability of capital to European firms. This stems not only from the surplus position of several continental countries, but, perhaps equally important, from the improved access of European firms to the international capital market. In the first quarter of 1969, for example, the new issues of non-U.S. firms shows a 90 per cent increase over the final quarter of 1968. The total volume of issues, $1.5 billion, was about twice the volume of the previous quarter; virtually the whole of this increase went to European corporate borrowers, mainly French, British, and Dutch; their borrowing now exceeds those of U.S. companies for the first time. It remains true that the U.S. capital market is virtually closed to European borrowers by the Interest Equalization Tax (IET). But this spectre too seems to be passing. The new Nixon Administration has reduced this tax, and its stated policy is to reduce it further. The confluence of interest rates throughout the world makes the tax less necessary, and borrowing on the U.S. market, in corollary, becomes less advantageous.

These developments may presage a new pattern of financial trade-offs between the United States and Western Europe. The past pattern, through 1967, is detailed in Table 4. It shows that while the United States and Western Europe each hold assets of about $21 billion in the other, the Americans have increased their direct investments to some $17 billion, and the Europeans, their holdings of shares and secondarily of direct investment to about the same amount. Preliminary data for 1968 indicated European asset growth to have outpaced the United States by some $1.4 billion net. The major elements here are European additions of $600 million in direct investment; $.13 billion in shares, an additional $800 million in the value of securities held, compared to additional direct investment of $1.25 billion by U.S. firms.

A final question relevant to trends and perspectives in international investment is that of growing concentration of international corporate power. A number of students believe that the world's economy of the future will be dominated by 300 or 400 superinternational corporations. It is, indeed, sometimes suggested that a global strategy must be adopted to join this chosen

TABLE 4

**Private Long-Term Investment Position of
the United States with Western Europe,
1950, 1958, 1965, and 1967
(in millions of current dollars)**

	1950	1958	1965	1967
United States Assets and Investments in Western Europe				
Long-Term Total	3,104	6,905	19,101	21,608
Direct	1,733	4,573	13,894	17,882
Foreign-Dollar Bonds[a]	85	244	823	718
Other Foreign Securities	409	974	1,973	2,148
Other	877	1,114	2,411	966
Western Europe's Assets and Investments in the United States				
Long-Term Total	5,299	11,389	18,342	20,247
Direct	2,228	4,070	6,105	7,004
Corporate Stocks	1,995	6,030	10,530	10,512
Corporate, State, and Municipal Bonds	123	136	654	1,440
Other	953	973	1,053	1,291

[a]Consists primarily of securities payable in foreign currencies but includes some dollar obligations.

Sources: Data through 1965 from *U.N. Bulletin of Europe,* Vol. XIX, No. 1, p. 66; for 1967, U.S. Department of Commerce, *Survey of Current Business* (October, 1968), p. 20.

group. This forecast is usually attained by an astonishingly simple route. Most of the large corporations have growth projections—7 per cent per year is a favorite one. If they grow at this rate and GNP grows at its expected rate, it follows that a vast percentage of future output will be handled by a relatively small number of companies. An alternative view, and one which we share, is that this is really not likely to happen. The relative division of output between small and large companies in the United States, where the integration process has gone on longest, has not really changed radically since the 1930's. Moreover, if one of the major motives for international investment stems from a company's holding some form of technological advantage, history indicates that standardized production, inviting numerous competitors, in time replaces even great technological leads. This simplified "product-cycle" concept is often difficult to see in current perspective, where strong emotions are involved. It is, therefore, of some historical interest that at the turn of the century, when the first U.S. investments began to frighten Europeans, *The American Invasion* published in England (the *Defi Americain* of its day) saw the giant and rapidly growing production of pig iron as the source of America's strength. This early talisman, forerunner of the computer, is today within the capability of any country willing to undertake it. When we admit that one man's crystal ball is as good as another's, this writer must remain iconoclastic about the prospects of the future super corporations. But the idea has had some use: The prospect of it has served, with great success, as a device for various national leaders to frighten their constituents about "monopolistic foreign domination."

We conclude this section with some definitions, as the ritual of briefing requires. With reference to the "international corporation," the term used in this volume, there are no standard, accepted definitions. The terms "plurinationales," "multinational," "transnational," or "international" company are used interchangeably. The Canadian Task Force Report distinguishes the national, the multinational ("sensitive to local traditions and respecting local policies") and the international corporation ("beyond the effective reach of . . . national policies . . . free to some extent to make decisions in the interest of corporate efficiency alone") but this division leaves most of the questions unanswered.[6]

With a few exceptions (Unilever, Shell, Nestlé) most international companies are still identifiable with their country of origin; managerial and even shareholding power, despite the financial crossover cited in this Chapter, are

---

[6] *Foreign Ownership and the Structure of Canadian Industry: Report of the Task Force on the Structure of Canadian Industry* (Ottawa: Prepared for the Privy Council Office, Queen's Printer, 1968). Throughout this volume, this study will be referred to variously as "the Watkins Report" and "the Task Force Report."

normally centered there. Time, transnational mergers, management selection on a geocentric basis, and further financial crossovers may change this.

Another dimension of definition emerges from some very incomplete data. An "international company" may be defined as one with foreign content of 25 per cent or more; "foreign content" is defined as the proportion of sales, investment, production, or employment abroad. Clearly, it would be preferable to use one of these criteria, rather than four interchangeably, but data are too scanty to permit this. By this definition, and restricting the base to the 200 largest U.S. and 200 largest non-U.S. firms (and excluding Japanese firms) in the *Fortune* 1967 list, there appear to be about 75-85 U.S., and a similar number of European companies which qualify. The lists appear in Tables 5 and 6. In the latter, British companies are vastly underrepresented, for lack of data. To repair this gap by yet another definition, Table 7 includes British firms with production units in six or more countries. An alternative British source appears in the Reddaway Report's list of companies queried.[7]

This listing is, to repeat, incomplete, and offered only as the broadest guide. It underscores the need for better data in this field, particularly as it omits virtually all smaller companies.

On the financial plane, some 20 U.S. and 20 European companies have listed their shares on two or more bourses. These companies are tabulated in Tables 8 and 9.

SOME HISTORICAL PERSPECTIVES

Most students of the international corporation emphasize the newness of the phenomenon. But the fact is that the internationalization of production and international corporate activity started at about the turn of the century. To select a wholly random example, Hoffman-LaRoche started to produce pharmaceuticals in Switzerland in the late nineteenth century; by 1908, it was producing in Germany, France, the United Kingdom, and the United States as well. Before the 1930's, IBM, Esso, Shell, Unilever, SKF, and many others were seasoned in the basic procedure, although strategies have changed over time.

But the movement toward internationalization succumbed in the interwar years to cartels, price-setting agreements and divided markets. Thus, for example, U.S. direct investment abroad totaled $7.2 billion in 1929; in 1946 it was still only $7.5 billion. When it reappeared in the postwar years, international

---

[7]W. B. Reddaway, in collaboration with S. J. Potter and C. T. Taylor, *Effects of U.K. Direct Investment Overseas. Final Report* (Cambridge, England: Cambridge University Press, 1968).

TABLE 5

American International Corporations, 1965

Rank	Fortune 500 Rank	Company	Sales	Earn-ings	Assets	Employ-ment	Produc-tion	Other
Foreign Contact Over Fifty Per Cent								
1	178	International Packers	96	––	55	––	––	––
2	148	Burroughs	––	69	43	––	––	––
3	3	Standard Oil (N.J.)	68	60	52	––	81	––
4	130	H. J. Heinz	––	65	55	––	––	––
5	214	International Milling	––	64	44	––	––	36
6	30	International Telephone & Telegraph	59	60	61	72	––	––
7	294	United Shoe Mach.	54	62	48	70	––	––
8	79	Colgate-Palmolive	54	––	41	––	––	––
9	61	Anaconda	––	54	36	––	61	––
10	453	H. H. Robertson	53	55	58	––	––	––
11	65	Singer	52	––	64	66	––	––
Foreign Content Over Twenty-Five Per Cent								
1	6	Socony Mobil Oil	49	52	43	51	76	53
2	89	Bendix	49	––	––	––	––	––
3	125	Chas. Pfizer	47	56	51	––	––	––
4	467	Standard Pressed Steel	––	47	27	––	––	––
5	167	Otis Elevator	46	35	29	––	––	––
6	418	Rheem Mfg.	46	32	41	––	––	––
7	92	National Cash Register	45	47	53	––	––	––
8	444	U.S. Industries	45	5	27	––	––	––
9	479	Dorr-Oliver	45	––	21	21	––	––
10	490	Mead Johnson	––	––	––	45	––	––
11	39	Caterpillar Tractor	43	––	19	17	––	––
12	66	Corn Products	43	47	43	68	––	––
13	228	Sterling Drug	42	33	30	––	––	40
14	308	Amerada Petroleum	––	––	––	––	67	––
15	116	Standard Oil (Ohio)	––	––	––	––	49	––
16	36	Phillips Petroleum	––	––	––	––	42	––
17	281	Foster Wheeler	41	64	42	––	––	––
18	296	Parke, Davis	41	30	23	––	––	––
19	391	Joy Manufacturing	40	––	33	––	––	––
20	252	Westinghouse Air	40	13	––	––	––	––
21	408	Chesebrough-Pond's	39	42	49	56	––	––
22	470	Black & Decker Mfg.	38	22	30	––	––	––
23	177	Warner-Lambert Pharm.	37	37	49	––	––	––
24	190	Dresser Industries	––	37	39	––	––	––
25	358	Rayonier	––	––	37	––	––	––
26	122	American Radiator & Standard Sanitary	36	57	37	58	––	74
27	475	Schering	36	56	50	48	––	––
28	287	Engelhard Industries	––	36	38	––	––	––
29	17	Standard Oil of Calif.	35	43	9	29	69	––
30	8	Texaco	35	25	––	––	65	––
31	203	Gillette	––	35	40	59	––	––

Rank	Fortune 500 Rank	Company	Sales	Earn-ings	Assets	Employ-ment	Produc-tion	Other
32	434	Cabot	--	35	14	25	--	--
33	183	Crane	--	35	10	--	--	--
34	59	W. R. Grace	34	--	--	--	--	--
35	20	Goodyear Tire & Rubber	--	34	40	--	--	--
36	208	Merck	33	31	42	--	--	--
37	266	Crown Cork & Seal	--	33	54	--	--	--
38	120	United Merchandising & Manufacturing	--	33	32	--	--	--
39	159	Ingersoll-Rand	33	--	--	--	--	--
40	209	Cerro	33	--	--	--	--	--
41	254	Norton	33	16	27	42	--	--
42	304	Richardson-Merrell	33	--	23	--	--	--
43	436	Wm. Wrigley Jr.	--	33	23	--	--	--
44	319	Electric Storage Battery	--	32	22	--	--	--
45	314	Carborundum	--	--	32	--	--	--
46	385	Ampex	32	22	22	20	15	--
47	9	IBM	30	30	32	36	--	--
48	495	AMP	30	25	30	35	30	30
49	230	Libby, McNeill	30	18	18	15	--	--
50	35	Eastman Kodak	30	15	28	37	--	--
51	60	Minnesota Mining & Mfg.	30	--	--	40	--	--
52	172	Clark Equipment	30	13	25	--	--	--
53	49	United States Rubber	--	--	30	--	--	--
54	141	American Metal Climax	--	30	9	--	--	--
55	253	J. I. Case	29	--	44	--	--	--
56	10	Gulf Oil	--	29	33	--	76	--
57	21	Union Carbide	29	22	17	43	--	--
58	46	Sperry Rand	28	--	42	--	--	--
59	286	Abbott Laboratories	28	--	30	--	--	--
60	19	International Harvester	28	19	26	32	--	--
61	415	St. Joseph Lead	--	28	--	--	--	--
62	31	Firestone Tire & Rubber	--	26	--	--	--	--
63	91	Reynolds Metals	26	--	--	--	--	--
64	277	Revlon	--	--	26	--	--	--
65	431	Chicago Pneumatic Tool	--	--	26	--	--	--
66	161	Johnson & Johnson	25	25	27	40	--	--
67	370	Harsco	--	25	27	--	--	--
68	5	Chrysler	25	--	26	24	22	--
69	52	Dow Chemical	25	--	--	--	--	--
70	488	Harnischfeger	25	--	5	--	--	--

Source: Nicholas K. Bruck and Francis A. Lees, "Foreign Investment, Capital Controls, and the Balance of Payments," *The Bulletin,* No. 48-49 (New York University, 1968), pp. 83-85.

TABLE 6

Some European International Companies[a], 1967

Industry / Country	Chemicals, Pharmaceuticals, Fibers, Rubber	Food and Tobacco	Oil and Extractive	Machinery including Autos	Electric Equipment	Glass, Metal and Miscellaneous
France	Rhone-Poulenc, Michelin, L'Air Liquide, Roussel		Cie. Francaise des Petroles	Renault Citroen	CSF[b]	St. Gobain, Pechiney, Ciments Lafarge
Holland	AKU-ENKA	Unilever	Shell		Philips	
Switzerland	CIBA, Hoffman-La Roche, Geigy, Sandoz	Nestlé		Sulzer Brown-Boveri		Alusuisse
Sweden				Alfa-Laval	Ericcson ASEA	SKF
Belgium	Solvay		Petrofina			Cockerill-Ougee
Germany	Bayer, Hoechst, BASF			Volkswagen Daimler-Benz Bosch	AEG-Telefunken Siemens	
Italy	Montecatini-Edison, Snia Viscosa, Pirelli			Olivetti		
United Kingdom	Dunlop, Courtaulds, ICI	British American Tobacco	British Petroleum, Rio-Tinto			Bowater

[a]Twenty-five per cent (+) of assets, earnings, employees, or sales (excluding exports from home country) abroad.

[b]Since merged with Thomson-Brandt.

Source: Special tabulation from annual and special reports and interviews.

20

TABLE 7

United Kingdom Companies with Six or More Production Facilities Abroad, 1967

Chemicals, Pharmaceuticals, Fibers, Rubber	Food and Tobacco	Oil and Extractive	Machinery, Including Autos	Electrical Equipment	Glass, Metal, and Miscellaneous
Albright & Wilson	British-American Tobacco	British Petroleum	Leyland-B.M.H.	English Electric	British Insulated Callenders Cables
Imperial Chemical Industries	Distillers	Burmah Oil	Joseph Lucas (Industries)	Associated Electrical Industries	Reed Paper Group
Courtaulds	Imperial Tobacco	Rio Tinto Zinc		Electric & Musical Industries	Tube Investments
Dunlop	Reckitt & Colman Holdings			General Electric	Bowater Paper
Coats, Paton	J. Lyons				Johnson-Mattey
Turner & Newall	Brooke Bond				Associated Portland Cement
British Oxygen					Dickinson-Robinson Group
					Guest, Keen & Nettlefolds
					Vickers
					Wiggens Teape
					Metal Box
					Delta Metal
					Pilkington Bros.

Source: Special tabulation from company reports and *Exchange Telegraph Service,* selected from British-based companies on *Fortune's* "200 Largest Non-U.S. Companies" list.

TABLE 8

Shares of European Companies Quoted in at Least Two Other European Countries[a]

Home Country	Company	Amsterdam	Brussels	Paris	Luxembourg	Frankfurt or Dusseldorf
Germany	AEG	—		—		
	Hoechst	—	—	—		—
	Rheinische	—		—		
	Siemens & Halske	—	—	—		—
Belgium	Cockerill-Ougree	—		—		
	Cofinundus	—		—		
	Gevaert	—		—		
	Wagon-Lits	—		—	—	
France	Banque de Paris et des Pays-Bas	—	—			
	Pechiney	—	—			—
	Peugeot	—	—			—
Italy	Montecatini	—	—	—		—
	Pirelli	—	—	—		—
	Snia Viscosa		—	—		—
Luxembourg	Arbed	—	—			—
Netherlands	Philips Gloeilampen		—		—	—
	Robeco		—			—
	Royal Dutch		—	—	—	—
	Unilever		—	—	—	—

[a]No foreign shares are quoted in Milan.

Source: Etienne-Sadi Kirschen, with Henry Simon Bloch and William Bruce Bassett, *Financial Integration in Western Europe* (New York and London: Columbia University Press, 1969), pp. 55-56.

TABLE 9

American Shares Quoted in at Least Two European Stock Exchanges[a]

Company	Brussels	Paris	Amsterdam	Frankfurt or Dusseldorf
Aluminum Co. of America (Alcoa)	--			--
American Tel. & Tel.	--	--		--
Dow Chemical	--		--	
du Pont de Nemours	--	--	--	--
Eastman Kodak	--	--	--	--
Ford Motor	--	--	--	--
General Electric	--	--	--	--
General Motors	--	--	--	--
Goodyear Tire & Rubber	--	--	--	--
International Business Machines (IBM)	--	--	--	
International Tel. & Tel. (ITT)	--		--	--
Standard Oil Co. of New Jersey	--	--	--	--
U.S. Steel	--		--	--
Union Carbide Corp.	--		--	
Westinghouse Electric	--		--	
National Biscuit		--	--	
Kennecott Copper		--	--	--
Socony Mobil Oil		--	--	
Merck		--	--	
Monsanto Chemical		--	--	
Procter and Gamble		--	--	
Gillette Co.		--	--	
Philip Morris		--	--	

[a]No foreign shares are quoted in Milan.

Source: Etienne-Sadi Kirschen, with Henry Simon Bloch and William Bruce Bassett, *Financial Integration in Western Europe* (New York and London: Columbia University Press, 1969), pp. 55-56.

direct investment changed from an important statistic to an avalanche in a single decade.

Consequently, to a generation of students trained in the interwar years, or weaned on books of the time, the phenomenon appears new, which it is not. And the same students, using easily available American data, and only attracted to the phenomenon from the late 1950's, a decade· dominated by American investment, have tended to believe direct foreign investment is an American phenomenon, which it is not. On the contrary, the data earlier presented suggest a rough conformity between the magnitude of direct investment and national capability—as evidenced by comparative GNP. The rush of U.S. investment in the decade may equally reflect an equilibrating move between those magnitudes on the Americans' part, for understandable reasons, and one now fated to flow. In comparison, a slower, more steady but again renascent outward movement has come from European centers.

Let us now turn to a key question: Why did the march toward internationalization stop from roughly the 1930's until the 1950's? There is never a single answer to a piece of economic history. Obviously the depression, autarky, World War II, and postwar uncertainties were all contributing factors to retraction. But if there is a single, most important reason to explain the outward push of U.S. investment in the 1950's, it would seem to be the impact of antitrust laws on U.S. industry. One branch of these laws was forged in the 1930's and 1940's precisely to fight cartels and international agreements. Consequently, at least for U.S. corporations, such agreements were illegal after the war, and prosecution was vigorous. It is true that the opening of economic space in the Common Market, rising standards of living, government encouragement of foreign investment, the Americans' loss of awe of their European counterparts, and the competitive spirit of U.S. management were also relevant factors. But all seem to have been eclipsed by the overriding importance of the legal mold into which U.S. antitrust practice pushed corporate behavior.

In Chapter 3, Mr. Ellis emphasizes the shortcomings of these antitrust procedures, particularly in their extraterritorial application and in their potential impact on European direct investors. The evidence is not unequivocal, however. He also indicates that the courts are less zealous in their defense of the "effects" doctrine, bowing increasingly to foreign law or even policy expressions, which thus effectively shield the foreign company. In Chapter 4, Dr. Damm suggests, as does the effective investment of over $7 billion by Europeans by 1967 and an additional $600 million in 1968, that much of the danger of antitrust action may be exaggerated. "The problems raised by extraterritorial application of U.S. legistlation and fiscal regulations become somewhat less acute once a subsidiary is set up."

It will fall to more competent hands to reply in legal terms to Mr. Ellis. Nevertheless, a few observations relating to the economic role of antitrust may serve perspective purposes here.

The U.S. penchant for antitrust stems only secondarily from a preference for competition per se, as Mr. Ellis suggests. It stems primarily from the political theory that unbridled monopoly is an abuse, the only rectification of which ultimately lies in some form of nationalization or socialism, a cure worse than the disease. The realistic alternative, which antitrust has by and large achieved, is to permit the creation of genuinely competing oligopolistic units. These are capable simultaneously of supplying many, probably most, of the benefits that competition brings to a society while at the same time taking advantage of the economic and technological efficiencies of modern production within a large market. Recent statements by prominent legal and economic spokesmen leave little doubt that the United States is not inclined to reduce its belief in the basic validity of antitrust procedures, even though every U.S. student of the problem is fully aware of the administrative difficulites and of the occasionally quixotic nature of their application.

Nor is this perception of the antitrust procedures entirely limited to the United States. The Rome Treaty (particularly Articles 85 and 86) contains provisions which might lead to a somewhat similar pattern. Certain regulations under the provisions, notably Regulation 17, form a basis for actions by the commission which for the period 1962-65 seemed to corroborate this tendency. Economic integration and the commission's active role have been severely slowed—whether permanently or not remains to be seen. But the complete picture of an integrated Europe, including transnational corporate mergers and a capital market unified either *de jure* by laws and tax harmonization, or as now seems more likely, *de facto*, by the increased interpenetration of the national and international capital markets, the latter too big and effective to be any longer considered a "substitute market," could well create in Europe much the same economic pattern the United States now has. A large market and the creation of big, technically efficient producers which must not be allowed to abuse a dominant position are strikingly similar to the economic ingredients of the U.S. antitrust policy.

The similarities cannot be pressed too hard. Profound differences will remain under any circumstances. Nor should the likely speed of such developments be exaggerated. But such a development is neither impossible nor even unlikely, unless integration is doomed to ultimate failure. And if it should transpire, the U.S. fear of a foreign by-pass to its competitive regulations would substantially lessen, and with it, the need for the "effects doctrine" and extraterritoriality.

The Canadian Task Force Report is often cited correctly as one of the purest *cri de coeur* against the excesses of U.S. extraterritoriality. Yet, with respect to antitrust laws, that report suggested that part of the failure in the relationship—and one of Canada's troubles—was the local failure to perfect and use "anticombination" laws.

In the interim, some retraction of extraterritoriality is taking place through the changed views of the U.S. courts, as earlier cited. Certainly for would-be European investors in the United States, clarification of administrative procedures, as Chapter 3 also suggests, is in order. One of the purposes of the Washington Conference should be to elicit views on the best methods to do this.

THE CONSEQUENCES OF INVESTMENT BEYOND BOUNDARIES

Two major sets of consequences emerge from the extension of corporate production across borders. The first set is economic consequences and is held almost universally to be beneficial. The second set is phrased in political or emotional terms; this includes the threat—often more apparent than real, but nevertheless action provoking—which foreign investment poses to local autonomy, or sovereignty, or control. Here politics and human feelings rather than economics are involved. Economic benefits and political or emotional costs are difficult to compare. They are denominated in different coin. When he speaks of Canada, the major author of the Task Force Report states the dilemma, which in fact applies to all nations:

> Canadian policy should be directed toward increasing the benefits from foreign direct investment and decreasing the costs. It is impossible to measure benefits in a precise way. There is always the problem that benefits are mostly economic while costs are political. How do you compare apples and oranges?[8]

Let us then separate the apples from the oranges and examine each in turn. The economic benefits of international production lie in the process of economic integration, here examined. The political costs give rise to the national response, to which the final section of this Chapter turns.

The motive of the international corporation is the search for reasonable profits. To obtain them, it seeks to locate its production and marketing operations wherever resources can be most effectively utilized, even across national boundaries. The major consequence of this activity is to promote economic integration. That is, international investment has spread, over the uneven economic landscape of the developed world, something approaching

---

[8]Melville H. Watkins, "Impact of Foreign Investments: The Canadian—U.S. Case," *Columbia Journal of World Business* (March- April, 1969), p, 25.

equality of wage and interest rates, products, technological and managerial skills. As the Rome Conference concluded, the international corporation has been a key factor in the virtual elimination of the so-called technological gap; indeed, the best way to establish such a gap would be to restrict international investment.

This integration procedure is not new. In earlier years, much the same thing occurred as the result of interregional investment within the nations. To use a U.S. example, during the 1920's and 1930's national companies and retail chains spread from the regions of their origin throughout the nation. They were able to do so because they effectively undersold local producing units or "Ma and Pa" stores, symbols of self-reliant localism—at a price. What the national companies were in fact doing was to provide better and cheaper goods to the market, higher ratios of capital to labor in production, hence, higher productivity and wages. In addition, bigness meant the national firms had central access to credit markets, advanced research, and professional management. Given a competitive framework, these benefits were spread to consumers, employees, and shareholders; and the business of managing became a lucrative seat of power and a career open to talents, attracting able men.

To be sure, there were oranges among the apples. The local response was highly emotional and deeply felt. The local shopkeeper and manufacturer saw the intrusion of alien companies as menacing in its undercutting economics and in its threat to proletarize the local factory or shopowner. The issues then, as now, were local control versus economic efficiency, via integration. But in fact small business has survived and occupies much the same economic position as it did at the outset of this process. This even tends to be true with respect to manufacturing, a function of the product cycle to which earlier allusion was made. In the all-important field of innovation, small business has come to occupy a position of such importance that capital-market funds are available for the development of new ideas.

If we may be permitted an analogy used before, in the earlier period Du Pont learned that it could organize its productive facilities, its money flows, its marketing, its managing elite, 3,000 miles west of Delaware. In the postwar period, the vision was extended: If 3,000 miles west of Delaware, why not 3,000 miles east? There is in fact no reason. And if Du Pont can do it, why not BASF, ICI, or Rhone-Poulenc? This is in fact what is happening. Economic integration, carried out earlier on the national scene not only in the United States but in other nations as well, has been moved to the international scene. Charles Kindleberger has stated this succinctly:

A case can be made that the development of the large international corporation in the 20th century will prove in the long run to be a more effective device for equalizing wages, rents, and interest rates throughout the world than trade conducted in competitive markets by small merchants. The analogy is with the national corporation which in the United States after about 1890 helped to equalize wages, interest rates, and rents within the country's borders by borrowing in the cheapest market (New York) and investing where it was most productive in terms of costs and markets. The resultant movement of capital and shift in demand for labor was probably more effective in, say, raising wages in the South and lowering interest rates there than either trade by local companies or the limited direct movement of factors.[9]

The foreign-investment process produces economic benefits to both capital senders and receivers. The cost-benefit analysis can get long and technical: Perhaps it can be stated briefly.

To the host country, there is a net addition to output which is always greater than the investing company's earnings, remitted or unremitted. If one assumes competitive conditions, an inflow of foreign investment raises the marginal productivity of labor and decreases the return to capital. Even if the returns to the foreign investor are equal to his marginal product, national income must exceed these earnings because the additional investment will have lowered the earnings of capital in general—both domestic and foreign. It follows that the larger the prior foreign investment, the greater the redistribution of earnings away from foreign capital to the domestic factors.

Even if one drops the often unrealistic assumption of competitive conditions, and therefore decreasing marginal productivity of capital, the foreign investor must still contribute more than he takes out because of the tax effects. An additional unit of foreign capital, even under monopolistic conditions, is likely to earn only about one third to one half of the net addition to national product resulting from its employment. This only considers the tax effect. It does not take into account the future growth in national output because of the percolating effect of external economies and the dissemination of know how.

This brief summary does not do full justice to the cost-benefit analysis, although more extensive analyses do not change the basic conclusions.[10]

To the investing company, the benefits are many: efficiency, getting behind tariff barriers, penetration of markets, and so forth. To the investing country, the benefit lies in profit remittance, i.e., in the balance-of-payments account. In

---

[9]Charles Kindleberger, *International Economics* (Homewood, Ill.: Richard D. Irwin, Inc., 1968), p. 400.

[10]See, for example, J. Dunning, "The Cost and Benefits of Foreign Direct Investment to the Investing Country, The U.K. Experience" (forthcoming article).

the United States, these totaled the $61.6 billion between 1950 and 1967, an amount equal to all foreign direct investment and the largest inflow item to the balance-of-payments account. In the United Kingdom, the exhaustive Reddaway Report[11] concludes that overseas investment yields to the economy a real rate of return about double the rate were the same money invested domestically, that foreign investment is not carried out at the expense of domestic investment, and that the average act of direct investment strengthens the future British balance-of-payments account.

But does the investing country not export its export base and actually lose balance-of-payments income because goods produced abroad would otherwise be exported? Various attempts to examine this question[12] have come to no conclusion. If company A did not produce in country B, would it *surely* export the same goods to B? Probably not: Others might export there instead, or the market might well never develop. The judgment of businessmen is that they could not in fact hold markets by exports alone, hence production in B.

Why then have both the United States and the United Kingdom tried to curtail the process? Officials in both countries concede the long-run benefit of foreign investment. But, they argue, curtailment of outflow in any one year produced a so-called cash benefit to the balance-of-payments account in the short run. The official apologia inevitably then relapses to the short-term ("crisis" is a favorite word) argument. What is a short run? The argument has been used since 1963 in the United States and much longer in the United Kingdom. Luc Wauters reminds us of a French proverb: "Il n'y a que le provisoire qui dure" ("only the temporary lasts"). This policy may well be changing now, at least in the United States, and so to attack it may be beating a dead horse. But it is difficult to avoid the observation that if British, and recently American, experience prove nothing else, they prove that there is no real dichotomy between the short and long run; the long run starts now, and once started on the wrong foot, it becomes increasingly difficult to shift step.

THE NATIONAL RESPONSE

In Chapters 5 and 6, Drs. Powrie and Hellmann deal with the national

---

[11] Reddaway, *op. cit.*

[12] G. C. Hufbauer and F. M. Adler, *Overseas Manufacturing Investment and the Balance of Payments*, U.S. Treasury Department Tax Policy Research Study No. 1, 1968. For reply, c.f., J. Behrman, *Direct Manufacturing Investment, Exports and the Balance of Payments*, (New York: National Foreign Trade Council, 1968).

response of Canada and Western Europe respectively, in admirable fashion.

It is readily apparent that the Canadian response is a special case when one considers the relatively huge proportion of investment that is foreign, and specifically from the United States, Canada's proximity to the United States, the ease of interchange between the two countries, and the imbalance in the sizes of the two economies. As Premier Trudeau put it:

> Living next to you is in some ways like sleeping with an elephant.
> No matter how friendly or even tempered the beast ... one is
> affected by every twitch and grunt.

In essence, the Canadian problem with foreign investment is not economic but political. One recent Canadian estimate suggests that without foreign investment, Canada would need to find an additional $3 billion of exports per year (compared to its $11–12 billion total presently), or suffer a contraction in its living standards. The real relevance of the Task Force Report, as Melville Watkins puts it, is "that Canadian nationalism, although weak, is real."[13]

Dr. Hellmann implies in Chapter 5 that the Continental Europeans have had to face the "apples and oranges" problem less severely than others because the proportion of their output which is accounted for by foreign investment is very much smaller and threatens the concept of national sovereignty, if at all, only in short outbursts of journalistic alarms. He also stresses the sophistication of the Europeans in emphasizing economic benefits and even in wishing to induce technological flows when capital inflow is no longer involved.

The reactions of the United Kingdom and Japan as capital receivers also merit brief comment. Writing on the case of England, John Dunning took a somewhat different tack. While he noted that U.S. affiliate output constituted about 10 per cent of total output) but some 17½ per cent of exports, and similarly noting other economic benefits to the United Kingdom from this investment, he nevertheless called for a continued surveillance of the procedure lest it get out of hand and threaten national sovereignty.[14] This suggests that the determining factor in evoking "oranges" may well be the proportion of foreign investment in the total national mix. And the implicit message from all of these analyses is that economic benefits are desirable so long as they remain sufficiently small or invisible not to threaten the perception of national control or to arouse psychological fears of domination.

Although it must be handled inadequately, some mention should be made

---

[13]Watkins, *op. cit.*

[14]John Dunning, *The Role of American Investment in the British Economy* (London: PEP, 1969).

of Japan's unique response. In the postwar period ending 1967, foreign direct investment was a mere 6 per cent of the cumulative total of $5.7 billion of foreign capital from all sources, including loans and bond issues. This limited, foreign direct investment was of course due to the restrictive policy the Japanese Government adopted toward foreign investment in the postwar years. While restricting foreign direct investment, Japan aggressively sought out advanced foreign technology. Japanese firms entered into over 9,800 licensing contracts with foreign firms, for which they paid the sum of $1.46 billion. Policy has thus changed little since the Meiji period. The Ministry of International Trade and Investment recently collected data relating to foreign investment in Japan which indicate that the bulk of it is in the petroleum, chemical, and machinery industries. While petroleum, largely for historic reasons, is about 60 per cent foreign dominated, foreign corporations account for no more than 5 per cent of national sales of any other industrial group and usually considerably less. Under the OECD's Code of Liberalization, the Japanese recently indicated that they would open their markets to foreign investment, by successive relaxations of restrictions. The process began slowly, presumably to be completed by 1972. This move may also reflect the fact that the Japanese economy itself promises to become a major capital exporter, international production units having been established in such fields as electronics, automobiles, and shipbuilding, and in a number of extractive industries for the purpose of obtaining raw materials. It may also reflect, however, the fact that Japan is now at a stage where it must have more advanced technology to continue to grow and that such technology is only obtainable by the surrender of proprietary rights to it. Paradoxically, Japanese industry, backed by Japan's excellent educational system, is now also at the stage where it is producing leading technology which can be marketed by foreign investment and production abroad as well as by exports.

Because the mote in another's eye is always more visible than the beam in ours, a look at the politics of developing countries may afford some clarity in the trade off between economic benefits and political costs. The sensitivity of developing countries to "external control" or "foreign domination" is more intense but no different in kind from that of the advanced countries. To establish a degree of local "control" over the foreigners, the less-developed countries (LDC's) have often enforced joint venture or share-participation schemes on investors or assigned specific industries to the limbo of government operation. These schemes have served to create what investors call "a bad economic climate," to limit badly needed investment in the LDC's, and to reduce the foreign-exchange earnings of LDC's into the bargain. The political motives are understandable, but the economic costs ought to be made equally clear.

But the whole question of national response cannot be limited to what one nation or another has done in view of the promises and threats raised by international corporate investment. Although the question of national response is usually formulated in these terms, a recitation of the history of acceptances or restrictions of foreign investment is only one part of the story.

There is a much more fundamental paradox involved. International investment is a reflection of the development of technology, and if technology—internal in the corporations' discoveries and production adaptations and external in the ease of travel, communication, and administrative control—is at the root of the movement, it is a movement certain to grow ever more important with time and to challenge every facet of the established order—financial, cultural, and political—in the course of that growth. Few human institutions in the past have withstood the march of technology, and those currently extant are no less likely to succeed. There can be, and have been, periodic setbacks; the *démarche* of international investment from the 1930's to the 1950's has been cited. But the basic forces propelling internationalization did not succumb in this period, as a cursory glance at the data since shows. In retrospect, the history of our time is likely to be recorded as the conflict between ethnocentric nationalism and geocentric technology.

Nor is this a new problem. One interpretation of economic history would argue that at least since the Middle Ages man's technological capabilities have outpaced his social and political organizing ability. The compass, the gun, the steam engine, the jet, the computer, even the missile and the H-bomb are no more than stations on the technological way; more will come. So too have there been political way stations—the city state, the duchy, the confederation, the nation state, and now haltingly in several areas, common markets. As technology for trade or war pressed then-prevailing political boundaries, those boundaries have historically expanded to incorporate and use the new dimensions technology made possible. Wider markets, wider defense areas, mean wider political dimensions.

But the evolution has never been smooth or rational. The very names associated with the triumph of the nation—Joan of Arc and Garibaldi, Henry VIII and Elizabeth I, Luther and Bismarck conjure episodes of violent changes. Not only were the political transitions bloody, they were impossible until the affected elite and the general populace were psychologically prepared to abandon the old and adopt the new form, if need to at great cost. And new forms were adopted at uneven rates, almost invariably benefiting those who adopted them early.

To reduce this sweeping generalization to the dimensions of the problem at hand, the fact is that the international corporation and international investment are part of an international dimension of life which would seem likely to call forth some form of international political organization. But a contradictory and dominant theme of our times is that the world is not yet ready to abandon the nation state for a broader organization. On the contrary, after a brief flirtation with internationalism in the 1950's, nationalism has again revived. And this return may be wholly defensible. Neither the performance of the United Nations nor of any lesser supranational body has inspired the wish to fly to new troubles from those we know. Indeed the conclusions of Raymond Vernon on this score could prove prophetic:

> There is a stubborn life and purpose in the system of nation states, and there is a tenacious capacity on the part of mankind indefinitely to disregard the seemingly inevitable ... even when the apparent cost of the identity and control seems all out of proportion to its value ... The world may experience a period of revulsion from the international order before it is prepared to move on to a new international synthesis.[15]

In economic terms, the nation state is based on the idea, dominant at least since the time of Adam Smith and David Ricardo, that products move internationally but that factors of production do not, and that nations should specialize and export those commodities in which they have a comparative advantage. The purpose of this activity is to accrue a favorable balance of payments, i.e., a surplus in the ensuing round of imports and exports, and the purpose of a favorable balance is to acquire or hold gold. It follows, therefore, a few doubt the wisdom, that the nation state is the appropriate means of organization of economic activity and that it is a proper function of the state to police, control, stimulate, or even run "its" industry. Nor, after two centuries, is this intellectual apparatus of most economists, and more important of the small army of politicians, civil servants, and the laity, seriously questioned except by a handful of heretics.

But this form of heresy has, conceivably, increasing evidence to commend it. It is apparent that international production has far outstripped trade as the main channel of economic international relations in terms of size, or the rate of growth, or future potential. It is further apparent that the national response to the international investment procedure is geared to the national interest. The countries have asked of the international corporations: "Are you good or bad for our national rate of growth, our national exports, our national balance-of-payments surplus, our technological and managerial prowess?" If the answers are positive, so has been the judgment, at least from an economic criterion.

Lest it seem obvious that the nation should so judge the corporation, it might be pointed out that there are alternative judgments which have crossed

---

[15] Raymond Vernon, "Economic Sovereignty at Bay," *Foreign Affairs* (October, 1968), pp. 120–22.

various minds. It is possible, for example, to appraise the international corporation in terms of its contribution to a regional economy, not to a nation but to the community of which the nation is a part. If the growth of production consequent to investment takes place outside the nation, it nevertheless benefits the welfare of the citizens of the community conceived in the broadest sense. That investment may, to be sure, be bad for the nation (its immediate balance-of-payments position, for example) but still be good for the community. The community may be defined in any size. Surely Europe is such a community; it is defensible that the Atlantic Community is such a community; some would extend the cost-benefit analysis to the world community.

No single government administrator can afford to judge the performance of international investment on anything but a national basis; such are the terms of reference of his employment. Some administrators have permitted themselves to wonder whether the performance of the international corporation should not be judged more broadly than by its contribution to the nation at one time.

But with no accepted theoretical framework to guide these thoughts—no substitute for the world of Adam Smith, the world of exports, and the world of the nation state—such thoughts must remain mere speculation.

Nevertheless, in the years ahead, those involved with international investment are increasingly fated to cope with the dichotomy between the national good and the good of a broader community. And while the affinity of corporate executives to their own nation state is presently unquestioned, the fact remains that in the course of their work, they are creating a different dimension of economic truth which must sooner or later be reflected in the political mechanism to deal with it.

2

THE ECONOMIC ASPECTS OF EUROPEAN DIRECT INVESTMENT IN THE UNITED STATES

Walter Damm

INTRODUCTION

While there has been an abundance of literature on the economic and political aspects of U.S. direct investment in Europe, relatively little has been published on similar operations by European firms in the United States. In recent times, however, the subject has gained in topicality. In the United States, it is felt that such direct investment would strengthen the balance of payments through the inflow of capital and the domestic production of formerly imported products. In Germany, the government, the central bank, and prominent businessmen have made statements in favor of direct investment abroad, in particular, in the United States. It would relieve the tight labor market and reduce the over-all surplus of the balance of trade which, incidentally, is already in deficit with the United States. It is felt that a high export share makes the economy vulnerable and that one should copy the U.S. example of giving preference to foreign production. It is believed that only the presence of strong subsidiaries in the large, competitive, and sophisticated U.S. market will give European business the experience necessary to compete successfully with U.S. firms all over the world. An increase in European direct investment in the United States would also become an effective counterweight to the ever-increasing volume of U.S. investment in Europe.

In this chapter, we will try to analyze these questions. The author fully realizes how difficult it is to produce a fairly accurate statement on such complex issues in so short a time, for the situation differs widely from country to country, from industry to industry, from firm to firm, and from product to product. Generalizations are therefore risky, but time and space limitations made them inevitable.

The writer had the opportunity to talk to several firms having invested in or who were planning to invest in the United States, particularly in branches such as chemicals, pharmaceuticals, steel, the oil and electrical industries, transportation, and banking. We would like to renew our sincere thanks for the generous support given to us. At the same time, we would like to stress that we alone assume responsibility for this Chapter and that neither the firms nor the European Economic Community (EEC) Banking Federation are in any way bound by our statements, conclusions, or errors.

In the first part of the chapter, a brief description is given of the attitudes of the European and U.S. governments toward the export and import of capital for the purposes of direct investment and legal and administrative restrictions they impose in certain cases. The second part summarizes European experience of direct investment in the United States, by analyzing the volume of such investment and by describing the advantages of and obstacles to such transactions. A special passage is devoted to strategy for market penetration. In the final part, some suggestions are made on the action that might be taken on both sides of the Atlantic in order to increase the flow of long-term capital to the United States.

INTERNATIONAL DIRECT INVESTMENT:
THE SHAM LIBERALIZATION

The Situation in Europe

After World War II, European governments generally considered foreign direct investment as highly beneficial in terms of economic progress both for the donor and the recipient country. This explains why the efforts to liberalize capital movements were concentrated particularly on this type of transaction. In the EEC, direct investment abroad and foreign direct investment were liberalized unconditionally as early as 1960, subject only to strict escape clauses of the Treaty of Rome. In the OECD, a similar albeit less stringent undertaking has been given in the code of liberalization of capital movements.

The situation appears less favorable, however, when looking at the regulations and their application in detail, and the fact that there is no universally accepted definition of what constitutes direct investment is only a minor point. The escape clauses of the OECD code of liberalization of capital movements offer governnments many possibilities for avoiding the general obligations to which they subscribed, and in recent years there have been well-publicized cases in the EEC where governments have modified or prohibited direct-investment projects considered to be contrary to the national interest.

The motives for these restrictions are usually straightforward in the case of direct investment abroad. Governments fear that an outflow of capital may disturb the delicate state of the balance of payments or deprive the country of scarce capital urgently needed for domestic development; thus, they import exchange control or administrative restrictions on the outflow of capital and regulate the repatriation or profits as in France, Great Britain, Norway, Portugal, or Spain. In some cases, tax regulations discriminate against foreign profits which are taxed more heavily than domestic earnings.

Foreign direct investments in the capital-importing country raise a much more complex issue. On the one hand, the recipient country is aware of the benefits it derives from the influx of capital, technology, management know how, and employment possibilities. Many European countries therefore actively encourage foreign direct investment. On the other hand, direct investment implies an exercise of foreign control which the recipient country will hesitate to accept when it affects "key industries." In some European states, this attitude has generated mental reservations or restrictions to foreign investment not only via exchange regulations but also through the right of establishment. They have adopted special authorization procedures, openly or indirectly discourage direct investment, limit the presence of foreigners in the board of management or the amount of foreign capital, or simply exclude nonresidents from certain types of business such as banking, shipping, communications, hydroelectric power, or even the teaching of dancing. It may be noted in passing that many of these restrictions existed before U.S. investment in Europe became a well-publicized issue, but the growing influence of U.S. firms made economic nationalism more prominent. Not only U.S. but also European firms were to feel the repercussions.

The Situation in the United States

At first sight, the attitude of the United States differs fundamentally from that of Europe. The U.S. Government deliberately encourages foreign direct investment largely because of the beneficial effects on its balance of payment. A special program, "Invest in the U.S.," was brought into being in 1961 for the purpose of promoting joint ventures, licensing agreements, and other types of investment in the United States to manufacture products at home that were then being imported. A special office was set up in 1966 by the Department of Commerce in Paris to encourage European investment, and several states such as New York, Illinois, and others opened representative offices in Brussels or Frankfurt. There are two federal agencies designed to give special assistance to

U.S. residents and to foreigners wishing to invest in the United States, i.e., the Economic Development Administration and the Small Business Administration. On the state and local level, development organizations offer nondiscriminatory financial or technical assistance, feasibility studies, tax incentives, help in finding and developing plant sites, labor-training programs, and so·forth. Foreign direct investment in the United States is completely free from exchange restrictions, and there is no need to obtain governmental approval to insert the individual investment project into the framework of an overall economic plan. In certain industries, special subsidies or tax privileges are granted on a nondiscriminatory basis. There are no impediments to the remittance of profits, dividends, and interest, or the repatriation of capital. The regulations relating to the public offering of securities of foreign corporate issues are substantially the same as for domestic corporations.

Unfortunately, this shining escutcheon is tarnished in places. There are many restrictions not only to U.S. direct investment abroad but also on foreign investment in the United States, and this is true even though European direct investment in the United States has come nowhere near the same proportions as U.S. investment in Europe. In the first place, one should mention visa regulations. Not only immigrants but also visitors and "treaty traders" are in certain cases subject to U.S. military service. Treaty-trader visas are available only when the capital of the U.S. subsidiary is at least 51 per cent foreign; they may only be granted to nationals of a country of a parent company which does not help other companies with a multinational staff. Problems also exist when European firms combine to set up multinational subsidiaries in the United States. Immigrant visas can be granted only after long waiting periods.

Numerous regulations both on the federal and state level concerning foreign direct investment restrict the right of establishment. With respect to coastal or inland shipping, domestic radio communications, domestic air transport, the development of hydroelectric power or atomic energy, the leasing or exploitation of mineral lands, or the exercise of banking activities, there are federal laws which prohibit alien ownership or limit the percentage of capital in foreign hands. Federal laws require that if a firm is engaged in defense contracts, all of its officers must be U.S. citizens.

State laws impose similar restrictions on aliens. The regulations vary from state to state, but as a rule they prohibit or limit the exercise of certain activities such as fishing, mining, banking, insurance, the alcoholic-beverage industry, or medicine and law. Some states require that a specified number or percentage of incorporators or officers must be of U.S. nationality.

Finally, there are also private restrictions in the stock-exchange field that exclude foreigners from membership.

THE EUROPEAN EXPERIENCE

The Difficulties

Even if one leaves aside the legal and administrative difficulties that both European countries and the United States impose on direct investment in the United States, there are a number of economic or phychological factors which impede such transactions or make them difficult.

One should not forget that up to the late 1950's, Europe suffered from a general shortage of long-term capital and was forced to use the scarce resources for the reconstruction of its war-torn economies and the financing of its infrastructure. Later, impressive growth rates in the gradually evolving Common Market enticed both U.S. and European enterprises to invest their resources there rather than in the United States where economic expansion, at least up to the early 1960's, was punctuated by occasional slumps.

Most generally speaking, there is no point in investing in the United States when one does not have a product to sell at competitive prices, which will frequently be the case in the consumer industry where the economies of scale work are in favor of the U.S. producer. In spite of transportation costs and U.S. tariffs, high labor cost and high capital intensity in the United States often make production in Europe more profitable. The high cost of transportation for bulk goods inside the United States can only be overcome by highly efficient ocean transportation and distribution at the ports of entry. In many cases, the U.S. consumer does not want to forego the prestige of the label, "Made in Europe." The often considerable tax and financing advantages granted under European regional-development programs constitute a valid argument for producing in Europe. In certain cases, direct investment in Canada and even in Mexico offer an attractive alternative for market penetration in the United States. Finally, there are branches of industry in the United States that suffer from overcapacity on the U.S. market—it would be folly to try and penetrate them from the outside.

The first important barrier to direct investment exists in the field of U.S. trade policy. Prior to setting up a production unit in the United States, it is necessary to test the market via exports, but the vagaries of U.S. trade policy, coupled with high tariffs and administrative obstacles, make this difficult if not impossible for some industries. Technical product specifications may act in the same way because they may vary inside the United States and because European standards—which are not lower, merely different—are not recognized. This obliges firms to produce in small and uneconomical series resulting in high losses which later have to be made up by direct investments.

The second problem is that of cost and financing. The cost of penetrating the U.S. market via direct investment is enormous by European standards and frequently overtaxes the capacity of the individual firm, particularly if it is of medium size. As a rule, European companies do not dispose of the considerable savings seeking investment outlets which U.S. firms have available for investment in Europe, and the sums at their disposal do not go as far as when invested in Europe. The establishment of European banks is handicapped by federal and state regulations.

The financing difficulties that the subsidiary encounters are the result of its small size. The parent company must therefore help either by providing a guarantee—which means showing a contingent liability in the balance sheet—or by direct financing support, which is difficult to raise in the United States. The parent cannot borrow on the U.S. capital market or obtain term loans from U.S. banks for use in the United States because the Interest Equalization Tax (IET) is applicable. Loans by U.S. banks to the parent company for use in the United States are also restricted by the Voluntary Credit Restraint Program. The restrictions also apply to U.S.-located branches or subsidiaries if the loan aids that borrower in making new foreign loans inconsistent with the program or if the loan would normally have been made to the foreign parent company. New share listings of the parent company on a U.S. stock exchange are also handicapped by IET and by the New York Stock Exchange or the U.S. Securities and Exchange Commission (SEC) regulations, which require methods of presentation and accountancy quite different from those customary or obligatory in the country of the parent company.

If the parent company plans a rights issue and there are shares held by U.S. residents, such residents must be excluded from the offering unless the parent complies with the disclosure requirements of the SEC. Unless these conditions are met, U.S. holders may only benefit from the rights issue by selling their subscription rights outside the country, but they may not exercise them. The IET acts as a further deterrent. Difficulties with SEC regulations seem to exist when an exchange of shares is planned between a European and U.S. company. Parent companies also fear to be exposed to SEC regulations if a subsidiary issues bonds with the guarantee of the parent company.

The possibility for the U.S. subsidiary to "go public" is excluded in the critical initial phase because of lack of profits, and just as with U.S. enterprises in Europe, there is a reluctance to relinquish the close control which goes with full ownership of share capital. The U.S. subsidiary is unknown to the banking community who will ask for guarantees by the parent, but the latter hesitates to show contingent liabilities in its balance sheet.

There is also the very high cost of setting up a distribution and service network. To overcome these difficulties, affiliation, joint ventures, or buying up a firm have been recommended, as those are cheaper methods than building up a new organization and have the advantage of providing local coloration. But there are also difficulties. To take up a financial stake raises problems because the subsequent division of profits takes no account of the technical and managerial contribution to the local firm. Takeovers are a "meat-axe" approach. Joint ventures seem to be a success only as long as each of the parties is convinced of the partners' superiority in a particular field and as long as the partners work as equals in an atmosphere of mutual trust. Unless the U.S. partner has a share of at least 80 per cent, U.S. tax regulations make it impossible for him to incorporate the initial high losses in a "joint return" and thus benefit from a lower rate of assessment. Once profits begin to flow in, difficulties may arise which may result in a takeover by one of the partners.

The growing trend toward an extraterritorial application of U.S. laws and regulations constitutes the third major obstacle to investing in the United States. Not only antitrust legislation, which is dealt with in a separate chapter, but also other laws and regulations are applied to foreign companies when their U.S. branch or subsidiary is considered an "agent" of the parent company. This threat frequently prevents an effective integration of the U.S. subsidiary into the overall organization and forces the parent company to take elaborate precautionary measures in correspondence, visits, exchange of information, and so forth.

There are also fiscal difficulties. Such state and local taxes as sales tax, franchise tax, and property tax are quite important and confusing, at least in the beginning; they differ from state to state and are not covered by double-taxation agreements. If a subsidiary receives supplies from a parent company, the latter may find itself subject to U.S. federal and state taxes for the profits effectively connected with the conduct of trade or business conducted with the United States. Temporary residents in the United States are taxed there, not only on their U.S. earnings but on their worldwide earnings and capital gains. If the subsidiary obtains double-taxation relief, it may lose such relief because the parent is a non-U.S. company.

The U.S. system of labor-management relations is also a cause for hesitation. Companies fear they might have difficulties in training labor and that craft unions restrict the versatility of the workers employed.

European subsidiaries also seem to encounter obstacles in the field of stockpile programs, aid to underdeveloped countries, and defense contracts. For obvious reasons, companies are reluctant to elaborate on these points.

Finally, one should not forget that there are also psychological obstacles to investing in the United States. There is the understandable trauma of the consequences of World War II. One should also mention the difficulty of adapting oneself to a competition-minded, profit-oriented, and risk-taking economy, for European firms sometimes give priority to the social-welfare philosophy of job security rather than profits. There is the legal maze of common law and its diversity from state to state which creates the feeling that no step can be taken without consultation with lawyers. The continuous publicity given to U.S. superiority in technology, management, and finance generates the discouraging feeling that European industry, already hard put to sustain U.S. competition in Europe, would be unable to survive if it had to compete against U.S. industrial giants on their home grounds.

The Facts in Figures

When one looks at the numerous hurdles, one begins to wonder if there have been any direct investments in the United States at all. A brief reference to statistics may therefore be in order.

When one compares foreign direct and portfolio investment in the United States and in Europe, it is surprising to find that there is no significant "investment gap" to the detriment of Europe; indeed, there have been times when European long-terms assets in the United States surpassed those held by the United States in Europe. For instance, in 1950, European direct investment in the United States was $500 million larger than U.S. direct investment in Europe. Only as of 1965 had the United States gained the upper hand with long-term assets totaling $19.2 billion, while European assets amounted to $18.3 billion. In 1967, these figures had increased to $22.5 billion and $20.2 billion respectively. By that time, the composition of assets had shown a considerable shift. While roughly 75 per cent or $17.9 billion of U.S. investment is in the form of direct investment and the remainder in portfolio investment, the corresponding relationship for European assets is 33 per cent to 66 per cent. In 1968 alone, net foreign portfolio investment in the United States amounted to $4.166 million, of which $2.23 million was shares and $1.9 million, bonds (including Euro-bond issues). These figures seem to refute the claim that Europeans have a marked preference for liquid holdings.

An analysis of the figures of European direct investment in the United States is revealing in many respects, as shown in Table 10 and Table 11. The United Kingdom has invested almost as much in the United States as in the rest of Western Europe combined ($3.1 billion as against $3.8). Inside the EEC, the Netherlands is the undisputed leader with $1.5 billion, while Germany, with $318 million trails far behind and is only in a slightly better position than France ($265 million). Switzerland, too, has invested heavily in the United States, with $1.1 billion.

An industry by industry breakdown shows the predominant role of the oil industry, particularly for the Netherlands ($1 billion). For the United Kingdom, the most important investments are in finance and insurance as well as in the petroleum industry. Investments in manufacturing also figure prominently, and this holds true for Switzerland, where pharmaceuticals dominate.

The increase in the volume of European direct investment in the United States is largely due to the expansion of existing facilities. Only in the case of Germany, closely followed by Switzerland, do the statistics show a marked increase in investments to establish a new company.

It is of course legitimate to ask why there is such a disparity between the European countries. One explanation is that United Kingdom, Swiss, and Dutch investments survived World War II relatively unscathed, although there had been some United Kingdom disinvestment, while German industry had to start afresh at a time when the home economy had to be rebuilt from scratch and capital and foreign exchange were scarce, quite apart from the fact that it would have been difficult for a German firm to set up a U.S. subsidiary in the immediate postwar years. But there seems to be another reason: Recent studies show that when companies can rely heavily on self-financing, there is also high direct investment (United Kingdom, Switzerland, Netherlands), while in countries with a low rate of self-financing, overseas direct investment lags behind (Germany, France, Italy).

The Rewards

European firms which have invested in the United States are usually highly enthusiastic about the value of their presence on this market. True, the road to success is often very hard and difficult; but it is considered well worth the effort for both the material rewards in terms of profits and the intangible ones such as access to management know how and technology, quite apart from the satisfaction of having succeeded in the most advanced market.

In fact, the United States constitutes the world's largest market. The infrastructure is well developed; raw materials and energy are available at low cost. There is an efficient communications, distribution, and advertising system and the trade-unions do not pursue political aims. It is a very competitive market, with a high rate of economic, technical, and social change, where competition through innovation is welcomed by sophisticated and price-conscious consumers for whom novelty is a virtue. Such a market, both in its purchasing potential and the challenge it offers, cannot be ignored and constitutes by far the most powerful incentive to export and invest in the United States, particularly for those companies which are innovators in products or technology and need to have a base in all major markets where investment can build up a permanent source of income, as compared with the temporary benefit derived from licensing. Particularly in advanced technology, only the U.S. and European markets combined provide an adequate base for production and marketing.

TABLE 10

Foreign Direct Investments in the United States, Selected Data, by Country and Industry

	Value at Year End			Capital Flow						Earnings[a], Income[b], and Undistributed Profits					
				1966			1967[d]			1966			1967[d]		
	1965	1966	1967[d]	Total	New Investments[c]	Other	Total	New Investments[c]	Other	Earnings	Income	Undistributed Profits	Earnings	Income	Undistributed Profits
Total	8,797	9,054	9,923	86	89	-3	251	133	118	695	371	339	804	381	440
By Area															
Canada	2,388	2,439	2,575	2	25	-23	9	19	-10	133	77	80	146	84	80
United Kingdom	2,852	2,864	3,156	23	18	5	65	21	44	234	125	102	257	124	123
Other Europe	3,224	3,409	3,848	67	43	24	185	75	110	307	159	143	386	163	229
Belgium	175	193	228	10	—	10	18	—	18	9	2	8	23	9	17
France	200	215	265	8	3	5	26	2	24	10	3	7	26	12	16
Germany	209	247	318	28	36	-8	65	37	28	19	7	11	30	14	16
Italy	87	87	86	1	1	[h]	-8	2	-10	1	—	1	8	2	6
Netherlands	1,304	1,402	1,508	20	3	17	12	[h]	12	153	73	78	177	80	93
Sweden	215	217	239	-7	[h]	-7	3	—	3	18	7	10	14	7	7
Switzerland	940	949	1,096	7	[h]	7	63	34	29	89	64	23	102	36	71
Other Countries	94	100	109	1	—	1	6	—	6	8	2	5	6	3	3
Japan	118	103	108	-24	3	-27	-2	18	-20	14	7	8	12[h]	8[h]	7[h]
Latin America	161	177	176	14	—	14	-1	—	-1	4	2	2	2	1	1
Other Countries	53	61	59	4	[h]	4	-5	[h]	-5	4	—	4	[h]	[h]	[h]

44

	Value at Year End			Capital Flow						Earnings[a], Income[b], and Undistributed Profits					
				1966			1967[d]			1966			1967[d]		
	1965	1966	1967[d]	Total	New Investments[c]	Other	Total	New Investments[c]	Other	Earnings	Income	Undistributed Profits	Earnings	Income	Undistributed Profits
By Industry:															
Petroleum	1,710	1,740	1,885	−94	1	−94	8	h	8	214	81	124	237	90	137
Manufacturing	3,478	3,789	4,181	111	47	64	138	84	54	357	159	200	380	132	255
Trade	748	739	848	−39	9	−48	67	21	46	43	15	30	70	28	42
Insurance	2,169[e] f	2,072[e] f	2,193[e] f	64	—	64	36	—	36	76	76	—	85	85	—
Other Finance	f	f	f	13	9	4	−20	2	−22	7[g]	22[g]	−5	23[g]	20[g]	10
Other Industries	693	714	816	31	24	7	22	26	−4	−2	18	−10	9	26	−4

a"Earnings" represent the foreign share in corporate and branch profits.

b"Income" represents the amount distributed, after withholding taxes, as dividends, interest, and branch profits.

c"New Investments" represent the first reported capital inflow to establish a new company or operation in the United States and also inflows to acquire additional shares of existing companies.

dPreliminary figures.

eIncludes market revaluations of securities held by insurance companies.

fIncluded in "Insurance," above.

gEarnings and income paid by agency banks in the United States to foreign home offices have been excluded from direct-investment totals.

hLess than $500,000.

Source: U.S. Department of Commerce, *Survey of Current Business* (October, 1968).

TABLE 11

**Value of Direct Investments in the United States,
by Major Industry and Country, End of 1967
(millions of dollars)**

	Total	Manufacturing	Finance and Insurance	Petroleum	Other
All Areas	9,923	4,181	2,193	1,885	1,664
Canada	2,575	1,397	354	99	725
United Kingdom	3,156	1,009	1,189	612	346
Other Europe	3,848	1,660	569	1,160	459
Netherlands	1,508	388	41	1,021	57
Switzerland	1,096	744	309	––	43
Other	1,245	529	219	139	358
Other Areas	343	113	79	15	134

Source: U.S. Department of Commerce, *Survey of Current Business* (October, 1968).

The presence of a big potential consumer market gives the necessary stimulus to introduce low-cost mass production at the earliest possible moment. The buoyant consumer market has great importance as an incentive for innovation.

Among the other arguments in favor of direct investment is the fact that direct investment reduces the proportion of exports to the United States and decreases sensitivity to uncertainty as to U.S. trade policy. It helps to overcome high tariffs and such administrative obstacles as the Buy America Act, which becomes particularly harassing when public funds are involved. It makes the granting of authorizations by such governmental or technical administrations as the Food and Drug Administration or Underwriters' Laboratories easier and facilitates access to government contracts. Particularly when the customer is a business enterprise, he frequently wishes to have production on the spot which assures him of better quality control of the products whose characteristics are determined jointly by him and the seller. The customer will obtain firm delivery dates. Shipping, packing, insurance, customs clearance, and so forth are no longer a problem. With production on the spot, it is easier to cater quickly to particularities arising out of specific national environment. Thanks to local production, the firm overcomes the hesitation manifested in the face of an "off-shore producer."

There is also the argument that in order to have rapid and full access to U.S. technology, in terms of invention, research, and development, and the effective utilization of innovation, it is necessary to make a direct investment in the United States. That is, however, disputed on two counts. In the first place, there does not seem to be a general U.S. superiority in innovation which is borne out by the increased flow of technical information to the United States. Second, it is felt that access to U.S. technology does not require direct investment; market observation posts or licensing agreements are as effective and less expensive.

The final motive lies in the field of management. U.S. managers are highly conscious of cost effectiveness, are flexible to react to change, are consumer friendly, expansion minded, and above all market oriented. The eductional system and the protestant ethic make the average American more business minded than the European. Given the competence of his competitors, a European manager in the United States will gain valuable first-hand experience, particularly in marketing, which he will be able to use in his home country and when competing with U.S. firms in other parts of the world. For this reason, the U.S. subsidiary frequently becomes a training post for young management which sets in motion a dynamic element for further expansion of the parent company.

The Strategy

One of the most important preconditions to gain a foothold is the willingness to adapt oneself to the characteristics of the U.S. market and the U.S. mentality and to adapt one's strategy accordingly. It will not pay to try and transfer European experience to the U.S. market, because the functioning of the U.S. economy, both on the producers' and on the consumers' side, is in many respects fundamentally different from that of a European country where production comes first and the market second.

The second condition is a careful analysis of the market, both of its present potential and its long-range prospects. This is costly, but there are ample data available and specialized U.S. firms often furnish high-quality studies. It is important to take the U.S. market seriously and not consider it as a substitute market depending on domestic-sales conditions. The firm has to realize that demand from the United States may become so strong that a substantial part of domestic production will be taken up by it; U.S. production may thus become a necessity. If not, the firm may have to make substantial direct investment to make sure that there is a highly efficient after-sales service including the supply of spare parts. It must also be aware of the problems that arise once a company changes from being "tolerated" to becoming a market force which the established firms will try to put in its place.

The financial strength of the subsidiary will be analyzed critically and is a condition for setting up solid business relations on the U.S. market. The parent company will have to have the necessary financial stamina to weather the initial losses which may be total.

The decision for direct investment should not be taken hastily. The best approach is to discover a market gap that can be filled by a highly specialized and technologically advanced product. This is made easier by the very size and specialization of the U.S. market both for capital and consumer goods. The venture will be successful only if the product has a so-called personality, if it is well presented and packaged, and if delivery dates are short.

In order to solve the problem of distribution, it is advisable to carry out a "seed" investment in an area with high purchasing power which is located close to the major clients. This is encouraged by the fact that fiscal and legal differences make the U.S. market a composition of regional markets. Once the regional base is established, expansion on a nationwide scale becomes easier. If the product permits, one should also make use of the distribution facilities of mail-order houses or chain stores. Small- and medium-sized companies may not have the financial and management resources to create manufacturing facilities in the United States. In such cases, a production agreement with a local firm may be a useful alternative.

The problems raised by the extraterritorial application of U.S. legislation and fiscal regulations become somewhat less acute once a subsidiary is set up. This will also ease financing problems, because the company may wish to "go public," although this is relatively rare and may become expensive both for parent and subsidiary because of the harassment by lawyers initiating "derivative" or "strike" lawsuits supposedly in the interest of minority shareholders.

While sales organizations are frequently staffed by nationals of the parent company, management of the U.S. production subsidiary will usually be entrusted to U.S. nationals or long-term residents. Particularly in the case of smaller companies, it may be difficult to provide an attractive salary, stock options in the subsidiary being rare and stock options in the parent company uninteresting from the point of view of U.S. tax law. This can be compensated for by a generous pension plan, "key-man insurance," and so forth, which entails taking a long-range view of the existence of the subsidiary. For monetary and psychological reasons, however, U.S. managers often do not want to be transferred out of the United States and therefore cannot be used in other subsidiaries.

A PLAN FOR ACTION?

As we have already shown, direct investment in the United States is a difficult undertaking, carried out normally only by the financially stronger and expansion minded but not necessarily only the larger companies. The United States adopts a very liberal attitude to foreign direct investment in the capital-movements sector, and once established, a foreign subsidiary frequently enjoys more freedom of movement than the parent company has in its own country.

Nevertheless, one should not forget that numerous discrimitory regulations against foreigners exist in the field of trade and establishment. The extraterritorial application of U.S. legislation is also a serious obstacle. Domestic regulations applied to foreigners sometimes have unintended negative effects. For their part, Europeans mention valid economic reasons for not risking the tremendous outlay but also sometimes overrate the importance of obstacles which by human nature are considered more vexatory in a foreign country than similar ones at home.

Taken together, these reasons explain why one should not overestimate the balance-of-payment impact that new direct investment in the United States alone will bring for each of the capital-exporting countries. Similarly, it is probably illusory to consider European direct investment as an effective counterweight to the "American invasion" of Europe unless there is a drastic increase in the volume of European direct investment.

It may also be legitimate to ask whether one can consider the policy of U.S. business to produce overseas as a model for the highly export-oriented European states. Taken in a wider context, a higher share of overseas production will doubtless reduce their vulnerability to the vagaries of trade policy and should therefore be actively encouraged. One should not forget, however, that in the United States the relationship of exports to overseas production is the result of specific factors. Because of the wealth and variety of natural resources, the size of the market, and the sophistication of industry and consumer, the United States never had to develop exports on the same scale as Europe. In Europe, the close economic interdependence, intense trading relations, and the absence of a raw-materials base have brought about a high level of imports which in turn created an imperative need to develop exports.

When one has given negative or guarded replies to so many questions, one may wonder if it is really worth developing direct investment in the United States. The answer remains an emphatic yes both for the European and the U.S. sides. The United States would stand to gain by such action not only because of the favorable impact of direct investment on the balance of payments but also because of the economic advantages resulting from a larger European presence on their market. As far as Europe is concerned, one cannot ignore the highly positive reaction of the firms that have made a success of their U.S. venture. One may validly conclude that the direct experience of the U.S. market is relevant, indispensable, and perhaps even vital for companies wishing to succeed in the growing European market and wishing to maintain their status as world firms. Wherever possible, one should therefore encourage such ventures and make them easier by creating more favorable conditions in the United States and in Europe.

On both sides of the Atlantic, it is of fundamental importance that governments and the public accept the consequences of the international division of labor. The concept that key industries—however difficult to define—must be reserved to nationals is an outcome of autarchic military and economic thinking which is not justified in a genuine transnational community. The conflict arises because companies have continued to expand their area of activity while political frontiers have remained stationary.

As far as the United States is concerned, it would be desirable for the authorities to recognize that in European eyes the investment climate—rightly or wrongly—is not always considered a liberal one. This would permit a reassessment of policies and a study of those discriminatory government regulations and private restrictions that might be abolished. This holds true not only for investment but also for trade, since exports are an indispensable prerequisite for setting up a venture abroad. For example, visa regulations might be re-examined and applied more imaginatively, and European technical product specifications might be recognized.

However, in view of the fragmentation of the European economies, a great deal will also have to be done on the European side. A balanced flow of direct investment is possible only between relatively equal partners. It is therefore imperative that Europe make a determined effort to create a genuine economic entity. This entails the creation of a European capital market in order to provide European enterprises with an adequate financial base through the promotion of risk capital and the inducement of European investors to increase their investment in European companies. It also implies a revision of tax and company legislation to facilitate mergers and takeovers not only on a national level but also across frontiers. National mergers provoke a national identification with the newly created company, while transnational mergers have the advantage of creating a new market. Both national governments and European institutions should pay greater attention to the promotion of research and the effective utilization of innovation. Uniform patent legislation would be desirable. Everything that might be done to help European industry weather U.S. competition in Europe will also indirectly promote European direct investment in the United States. Governments should abandon their mistrust of direct investment abroad which is looked upon less favorably than exports. Firms should try to overcome the psychological handicaps of investing in the United States. Multinational groupings might be set up with a view to penetrating the U.S.

One might consider the creation of consultative bodies in Europe which act as central pools of information and help avoid the pitfalls awaiting the investing novice. A larger presence of European banks in the United States would encourage firms to invest there. The banks could act as a guide to firms, and through loans or guarantees, help them overcome the financing problems which they would otherwise encounter because they were unknown. With the larger companies, it might be rewarding to associate local capital by "going public." In the fiscal field, it would be desirable to avoid tax discrimination of foreign profits, to take into consideration the possibility of depreciating the initial losses of the foreign subsidiary or branch, and to create a network of double taxation agreements based on the OECD model convention.

But while governments can make the social and economic environment more conducive to foreign direct investment in the United States, their policy cannot take the place of the decisions of management. The risk can be diminished, but it cannot be removed. It is up to management to decide where to invest resources, based on a sober assessment of the present and future market and the likelihood of success.

CHAPTER **3** **THE LEGAL ASPECTS OF EUROPEAN DIRECT INVESTMENT IN THE UNITED STATES**

J. J. A. Ellis

Of the numerous legal aspects of European direct investment in the United States, we chose to deal here mainly with the extraterritorial application of United States antitrust laws. Then, we describe the legal insecurity in the setting up of joint ventures in the United States. Finally, the U.S. Securities Exchange legislation and regulations issued thereunder are discussed.

THE EXTRATERRITORIAL APPLICATION OF U.S. ANTITRUST LEGISLATION

An important legal problem connected with European investments in the United States is created by the extraterritorial application by the United States of its antitrust legislation. Foreign companies which make direct investments in the United States may become subject to the jurisdiction of the U.S. federal courts in antitrust matters. Thereby they become exposed not only to the application of U.S. antitrust laws with regard to their activities inside the United States (which is only normal), but also to the risk that the U.S. authorities will seek to apply these laws even to their activities outside the United States.

It is fortunate that we are able to discuss this subject otherwise than in the context of a particular case and that it is thus devoid of the emotions which customarily surround litigation.

When the American Law Institute was drafting its thesis on this matter, it asked and obtained the advice of a European advisory committee composed of highly authoritative European international jurists. The opinion of that committee on the question of the permissibility under international law of extraterritorial application of antitrust legislation diverged sharply from the theory underlying U.S. practice. A legal discussion would not be in accordance with the objects of this volume, but we ought to mention, however, that the rules adopted by the American Law Institute have not been accepted internationally, notwithstanding the eminent status of that body. It is unfortunate that the advice given by the European advisory committee was rejected on this important substantive issue.

On the international level, the international-law aspect of extraterritorial application of national antitrust laws is being studied by the International Law Association (ILA). A resolution pointing out that international law does set limits to the jurisdiction of individual states was accepted, over U.S. objections, with an overwhelming majority by that body at its Tokyo conference in 1964. The subject matter was discussed further at the Helsinki and Buenos Aires conferences of the ILA and will again come up in forthcoming conferences. In the meantime, European businessmen who desire to make investments in the United States are confronted with the practical risks to their non-U.S. operations which may result from their decisions to do business in the United States.

Let us make one thing clear from the beginning: There is no question at all as to the fact that everybody who performs any act in the United States must do so in conformity with U.S. law. Every businessman, U.S. or non-U.S. citizen, resident in the United States or abroad, is and should be subject to U.S. law regarding his activities in the United States.

The problem, once the U.S. courts find that they have jurisdiction over a company, either directly or through a subsidiary or affiliated company is that these courts at the same time arrogate unto themselves the power to dictate to that company what it must do and what it must not do outside the United States. The objective is usually to reorder and restructure the foreign enterprise in order to remove and to prevent in the future those activities outside the United States which may have an impact on domestic and foreign trade of the United States.

Let us interject here that the extraterritorial application of U.S. antitrust law is governed by the "effects" theory (i.e., the effects of acts performed abroad upon U.S. domestic or foreign trade) and does not depend on the nationality of the enterprise involved. There exists in this respect no difference in the treatment of foreigners and U.S. nationals.

In this chapter, we will discuss the subject under four sections: (1) the assumption of jurisdiction over foreign enterprises in antitrust matters; (2) the type of orders given by U.S. courts to foreign companies in relation to activities outside the United States; (3) savings clauses in U.S. court decisions; and (4) is there a solution?

The Assumption of Jurisdiction over Foreign
Enterprises in Antitrust Matters

By making direct investments in the United States, a European company can very easily become subject to the jurisdiction of the U.S. federal courts in antitrust matters. For that purpose, it is sufficient if a company is "found" in the United States or if it "transacts business" there. The following points of contact have, for instance, been held sufficient for the U.S. courts to exercise in personam jurisdiction over foreign companies in antitrust cases.

Scophony Corporation Limited, a British company, with a view to protecting its interests during World War II, transferred its patents covering equipment for television reception and transmission to its U.S. subsidiary, Scophy Corporation of America. It was agreed that the U.S. subsidiary would exploit those patents by granting licenses to interested parties in the United States. Contracts between the parent and the subsidiary companies created certain controls by the parent over the subsidiary. These controls, taken in conjunction with the stock control of the British parent company, put it in a position to supervise the subsidiary's affairs and to intervene in those affairs. The U.S. Federal Court found that the business of the British parent company and of the U.S. subsidiary could be considered as practically a common enterprise and thus held that the British company was transacting business in New York.[1]

In another case, ICI (London) was found in New York through its subsidiary there, ICI (New York). This subsidiary was the buying and selling agent of the parent company and negotiated contracts on behalf of the parent company. ICI (London) exercised control over it through the officers and employees of the subsidiary: The key officers of ICI (New York) were previous employees of ICI (London) and were still operating in New York under employment contracts with ICI (London).[2]

In the Swiss watchmakers case, several Swiss companies and a Swiss trade association were made subject to the jurisdiction of the Federal Court in New York for various reasons. Some of the defendants were considered to do business in New York because they owned a U.S. subsidiary, the Watchmakers of Switzerland Information Centre, Inc. The U.S. subsidiary was organized as part of a program to create favorable publicity for Swiss watches in the United States and to establish a source of watch-repair parts. The court considered that

---

[1] *United States v. Scophony Corporation* 333 U.S., 795 (1948).

[2] *United States v. United States Alkali Export Association,* CCH Trade Cases 1946–47, par. 57481; *United States v. Imperial Chemical Industries Limited,* 100 F. Supp. 504, SDNY (1951).

"realistically appraised the Information Centre has no business of its own" and characterized the U.S. company as a "mere adjunct of its parents and its activities will be regarded as theirs."[3]

Electrical & Musical Instruments Limited, a British company, was held to be transacting business in New York, because its American subsidiaries were found to be not "mere distributors" but "reciprocating partners" making substantial contributions to the parent's business. Under those circumstances the Court did not find it "unfairly inconvenient" for the British company to stand trial in New York.[4]

Siemens and Halske A G, a German company, was held to be subject to the jurisdiction of the U.S. courts on the basis of agency, because its U.S. subsidiary assisted the German parent by negotiating and servicing contracts, selling the parent's products, and furnishing technical and economic information.[5]

These are a few well-known examples taken from U.S. court decisions in antitrust cases. A look at other fields of the law makes it clear that under U.S. legal concepts the reach of personal jurisdiction over a foreign defendant can go extremely far. In another well-known case,[6] a nonresident insurance company became subject to the jurisdiction of the courts of the state of California under a California long-arm statute. The U.S. Supreme Court held it sufficient that the beneficiaries' suit was based on a contract which had substantial connection with California. The court pointed out that the contract was delivered in California, the premiums were mailed from there, and the insured was a resident of that state when he died; that California had a manifest interest in providing effective means of redress for its residents when their insurers refused to pay claims; that these residents would be at a severe disadvantage if they were forced to follow the insurance company to a different state in order to hold it legally accountable; and further considerations of the same type. On the basis of these considerations the U.S. Supreme Court recognized the right of the state of California to assume personal jurisdiction over the nonresident insurance company. In a comment on the decision, one authority wrote that even a single contract with a state may be sufficient as a basis for jurisdiction of an action arising out of that contract.[7]

It will be evident from the above enumeration that every European company which does make direct investments in the United States must take

---

[3] *United States v. Watchmakers of Switzerland* 133 F. Supp. 40, SDNY (1955).

[4] *Electrical & Musical Instruments Limited* 155 F. Supp. 892, SDNY (1957).

[5] *Siemens and Halske AG*, 155 F. Supp. 897, SDNY (1957).

[6] *McGee v. International Life Insurance Company* 335 U.S. 220 (1957).

[7] Moore, *Federal Practice*, page 1291.8.

into account that it may thereby become subject to the jurisdiction of the U.S. courts in antitrust matters and that it may thus expose itself to the extraterritorial application of U.S. antitrust laws to its non-U.S. operations.

The Type of Orders Given by U.S. Courts
to Foreign Companies in Relation to
Activities Outside the United States

Once having become subject to the jurisdiction of the U.S. courts, the European company would have to realize that the U.S. antitrust laws might at some time in the future be applied extraterritorially to its activities outside the United States. The administration of justice by the courts under these laws might take the form of criminal proceedings brought by the Department of Justice, so-called civil proceedings brought by the Department of Justice for injunctive and other equitable relief, or civil proceedings for (treble) damages brought by a private party. The so-called civil proceeding brought by the government usually causes the greatest concern for the foreign investor, as it not only seeks to stop certain practices in the United States but may also seek to reorder and restructure an entire enterprise or group of enterprises abroad in order to ensure that similar effects are not produced in the future.

To illustrate the type of injunction given by U.S. courts in antitrust cases in relation to the activities of companies outside the United States, a few salient cases are cited hereunder. These concern both non-U.S. companies and foreign subsidiaries of U.S. companies. Both types of cases are relevant in this enumeration, because they have not been decided on the basis of nationality or residence of the companies involved but on the basis of the effects of the activities of these companies outside the United States on the foreign commerce of the United States.

The manufacture of titanium pigment was based on three independent inventions: United States, Norwegian and French. National Lead and Du Pont each had certain rights with respect to these inventions. Having found that these two companies had used these rights for the purpose of dividing world markets, the courts directed them to grant nonexclusive licenses to any interested party under their patents (including the foreign ones), and the courts also ordered National Lead to divest itself of its interest in four foreign titanium enterprises.[8]

In 1928, Alcoa founded a subsidiary in Canada, Aluminim Limited; subsequently, Alcoa had distributed the shares of Aluminum Limited to Alcoa's

---

[8] *United States v. National Lead Co.,* 63 F. Supp. 513, SDNY (1945); 332 U.S. 319 (1947).

own shareholders. In the 1945 case, Aluminum Limited was summoned as codefendant with Alcoa. The position was that the Canadian company had joined a European cartel, embodied in the Swiss Alliance Aluminum Company. The European cartel had not fixed any export quotas with respect to Canada or the United States, but it had fixed production quotas. Judge Learned Hand, delivering judgment for a unanimous Federal Court of Appeals, held that the production quotas must be deemed to have had the same effect on exports to America as though export quotas had been fixed. That effect was not in fact proved, nor did it exist at the time of the judgment, because the European cartel agreement had become ineffective as a result of World War II. The court nevertheless held that, having regard to the nature of the agreement and the necessary consequences of the intention ascribed to the parties, the cartel must be presumed to have had an effect on the American import trade. Although the Canadian company argued that the agreement was no longer in effect and that the issue was, therefore, moot, the court held that it should be enjoined from taking any part in any similar cartel agreement in the future. In 1950, Judge Knox, because a number of large shareholders and directors of Alcoa also held shares in the Canadian company, ordered their shareholders with shares in Alcoa and Aluminum Limited to dispose of their shares in one or the other within ten years. Up to the time of such sale, the voting rights attached to the Aluminum Limited shares were to be exercised by a trustee. The effect of this judicial order was to divest the original shareholders of either the ownership or the voting rights of 51.6 per cent of the Canadian shares which carried voting rights.[9]

The American Timken Company held 30 per cent of the shares of Timken Limited, a British company, and 50 per cent of the shares of Timken Française, a French company. Between the American, British, and French Timken companies there were contracts providing for the allocation of sales territories, exclusive cross licensing, and the use of each other's trademarks. The lower court forbade American Timken to fulfull the contracts, so that it would have to compete with British Timken and French Timken on foreign markets. The court also ordered American Timken to sell all of its shares in British Timken; but the U.S. Supreme Court, although following the lower court on all other points, did not uphold this part of the judicial order, finding it "unduly harsh." To ensure competition with British and French Timken abroad, the U.S. company was ordered to publish the terms of the lower court's judgment and at the same time to announce that the restrictions which had hitherto prevented the U.S. company from selling its products abroad had been removed. The U.S. company was also ordered to advertise its own wares in those areas which had previously been allocated to the British or French company. The defendant company

---

[9] *United States v. Aluminum Company of America*, 148 F. 2nd 416, 2nd Cir. (1945); 91 F. Supp. 333 SDNY (1950).

contended that it could not export directly to a number of countries–in Britain and France this was impossible owing to protectionist measures–but the lower court rejected this defense because market sharing and price fixing had taken place between the Timken companies, which arrangements are illegal per se in U.S. internal trade; the lower court held that the same rule of illegality per se must be applied with undimished force to foreign trade.[10]

Du Pont, an American chemical concern, and ICI, a British chemical concern, had a cooperative agreement under which patents and technical information were exchanged and markets allocated. Under this agreement, a number of joint enterprises were carried on in various countries. The judgment in this case had four important extraterritorial aspects: (1) The exchanged patents had to be returned to the original holder and made available for licensing to any interested party; (2) the market sharing had to cease; (3) joint interests in Argentina, Brazil, and Canada had to be terminated by either Du Pont or ICI disposing of their shares in the joint enterprises; (4) ICI, a non-U.S. company, was given a direct order by the U.S. court to hand back to Du Pont the British patent rights it had acquired from the latter. The decision had important consequences, particularly with reference to a Canadian joint company in which, in addition to Du Pont and ICI, there was a Canadian shareholding of 17.4 per cent. Because of the even balance between the major shareholders, the Canadian shareholders in fact had a dominating position which they would lose if Du Pont or ICI were to get rid of their shares. Ultimately the joint company in Canada was in fact broken up and two separate enterprises formed; one, controlled by Du Pont, concentrated on the production of nylon and cellophane, while the other, controlled by ICI, produced other chemicals and plastics. The Canadian shareholders in the former joint company received 18 per cent of the shares in each of the two new enterprises. This interference with Canadian enterprises and with the rights of Canadian shareholders aroused a storm of protest in Canada.

With regard to the judicial orders concerning the return of foreign patents exchanged between Du Pont and ICI, difficulties arose in Britain. ICI had, via the exchange, acquired all rights to a British patent of Du Pont's and had given an exclusive sublicense under that British patent to a British firm, British Nylon Spinners Limited (BNS). According to the U.S. judgment, ICI was to reassign to Du Pont the rights in the patent concerned, and Du Pont was to grant nonexclusive licenses on that British patent to any interested party. BNS opposed this move, whereupon the English court restrained ICI from complying with the U.S. judgment, so that ICI was unable to reassign all the rights in the

---

[10] *United States v. Timken Roller Bearing Co.,* 83 F. Supp. 284 ND Ohio (1949); 341 U.S. 593 (1951).

British patent acquired by Du Pont. BNS was therefore upheld in its rights as sublicensee.[11]

In the following case, the court held that an agreement among British, French, and U.S. companies not to compete in each other's markets was illegal, enjoined the U.S. company (the British and French companies were not parties to the action) from further performing or enforcing the agreement, and ordered it to take certain affirmative action to compete with the two foreign companies. This included "reasonable efforts" to promote the sale and distribution of Holophane products in foreign markets, without, however, violating patent or trademark rights; the offering of products for sale in such markets; circularizing potential distributors in the territories of the British and French companies; and advertising in trade journals and circularizing persons who had made inquiries that products of the U.S. company were available for sale to such territories.[12]

In the following case, a District Court found that the basic agreements constituting the Swiss watchmaking industry, which had been in effect since the early 1930's, evidenced a "conspiracy" to restrain the commerce of the United States, that they did restrain such commerce, and that they were accordingly contrary to U.S. law. Before the Swiss Government had undertaken direct negotiations with the U.S. Government on the terms of the final judgment, the court had not only issued sweeping injunctions against the two main Swiss associations but had also directed its orders to Swiss entities which had never even been served in the case and provided that the decree applied to all persons in active concert with any defendant who had actual notice of it.

The decree imposed wide prohibitions on contracts made in Switzerland, governed by Swiss law and relating to the manufacture and sale of watches and watch parts in Switzerland to the extent that such contracts restricted production anywhere in the world outside Switzerland. It ordered all restraints on exports to the United States to be stopped notwithstanding the active support and participation by the Swiss Government in industry regulations which had been in effect for many years. Moreover, it ordered the Swiss defendants to "cancel, terminate, withdraw from or otherwise render inapplicable, to United States commerce" provisions in contracts between the Swiss industry and manufacturers in Great Britain, France, and Germany, notwithstanding that such contracts were not directed to U.S. trade but were negotiated by or with the support of the Swiss Government for the purpose of developing

---

[11] *United States v. Imperial Chemical Industries Ltd.,* 100 F. Supp. 504, SDNY (1951); 105 F. Supp. 215 (1952).

[12] *United States v. Holophane Co., Inc.,* 119 F. Supp. 114, S.D. Ohio (1954); Aff.'d 352 U.S. 903 (1956).

Swiss watchmaking interests in those countries. It also ordered sweeping changes in the bylaws of the Swiss Watch Federation to reorganize its internal structures which were considered restrictive of U.S. commerce.

After the Swiss Government had intervened directly with the State Department and the Department of Justice, important changes were made in the final judgment, including the insertion of a provision that nothing contained in it would limit or circumscribe the sovereign right and power of the Swiss Government to control or regulate its own domestic or foreign commerce or to apply regulations to the watchmaking industry. Nevertheless, the modified final judgment still contained broad prohibitions relating to contracts and other arrangements, including contracts with the British, French, and German industries.[13]

Saving Clauses in American Court Decisions

Unavoidably, the extraterritorial application of U.S. antitrust laws led to conflicts with other governments. Apparently, not all of the protests which have been ledged by other governments with the U.S. Department of State have been published. However, those which have form an impressive list and include protests made by the governments of Canada, Denmark, Finland, France, Germany, India, Ireland, Italy, Japan, the Netherlands, Norway, Sweden, Switzerland, the United Kingdom, and Yugoslavia. It is significant to note the persistence of these protests. This phenomenon is explained by the fact that the extraterritorial application of U.S. laws is considered to be an infringement of the sovereignty of the foreign countries concerned.

Governments have not, however, limited themselves to protests alone. A number of countries have enacted laws to protect themselves against interference by U.S. authorities in what they consider their internal affairs. Some of these laws prohibit compliance with any type of order emanating from a foreign state which relates to economic competition. Others forbid production of documents to foreign authorities, and others again are directed at the protection of a specific industry, viz, the shipping industry. Protective legislation of one or more of these types now exists in the following countries, most of them European: Denmark, Finland, India, the Netherlands, Norway, Sweden, and the United Kingdom, and in the Canadian provinces of Ontario and Quebec.

---

[13] *United States v. The Watchmakers of Switzerland Information Centre, Inc.*, Final Judgment (January 22, 1964), SDNY Civil Action No. 96–170, Modified (January 7, 1965), CCH 1965 Trade Cases 71352 SDNY.

A recent development in this field is the Watkins Report.[14] *Inter alia,* this report proposed to the Canadian Government the introduction of legislation prohibiting compliance on Canadian territory with any antitrust order by any foreign authority without permission first being granted by the Canadian Government.

Admittedly the U.S. courts have been inserting saving clauses in their decisions which exclude the requirement of acts abroad contrary to the law of the country where they have to be performed. Thus, in the General Electric (lamp) case, the court included the following in the final decree:

> Philips shall not be in contempt of this Judgment for doing anything outside of the United States which is required or for not doing anything outside of the United States which is unlawful under the laws of the government, province, country or state in which Philips or any other subsidiaries may be incorporated, chartered or organized, or in the territory of which Philips or any such subsidiaries may be doing business.

And in the consent decree in the antitrust proceedings against U.S. oil companies operating outside the United States, the court went further in providing that certain injunctions should not apply where participation in a prohibited combination was made

> pursuant to request or official pronouncement of policy of the foreign nation or nations within which the transactions which are the subject of such combination take place . . . and where failure to comply with which request or policy would expose Jersey to the risk of the present or future loss of the particular business in such foreign nation or nations[15]

Though saving clauses such as these offer relief in some instances, they are not the answer to the problem of protecting foreign companies against the application of U. S. orders to business activities in foreign countries. It is not enough merely to exclude from a U.S. decree injunctions that prohibit conduct abroad required by foreign law or to exclude directives requiring conduct abroad

---

[14]*Foreign Ownership and the Structure of Canadian Industry: Report of the Task Force on the Structure of Canadian Industry* (Ottawa: Prepared for the Privy Council Office, Queen's Printer, 1968). Commonly referred to as "the Watkins Report."

[15]*United States v. Standard Oil Co. (New Jersey),* CCH 1960, Trade Cases, Par. 69,849, SDNY (1960).

that is prohibited by foreign law. In most countries outside the United States there are few express legal enactments relating to restrictive agreements, and where there are, those do not usually contain the same prohibitions or requirements as those contained in U.S. law. In most instances, companies abroad are governed by the general law and by the policies of their governments, but the latter may not appear in any positive form. Apart from the consent decrees, in the case against oil companies operating abroad, U.S. court orders do not exempt foreign conduct on the ground of compliance with foreign governmental policies. It is true that in one well-known case[16] the court did say that the directives of a foreign government organ "should be given appropriate weight" and it did suggest that official protests might be heeded, but there does not appear to be certainty that another court would follow this lead, and even if there were, it would mean that the extraterritorial application of U.S. law would be dependent upon a political decision by a foreign government rather than upon the basis of a legal principle. It must be recognized that every political decision involves the weighing of factors unconnected with the particular case in question. For a foreign company considering whether or not to enter the United States and thereby to risk the application of U.S. law to its activities outside the United States, such a basis for the administration of justice by the U.S. courts would not offer any reasonable degree of security for its future operations in other countries.

Is There a Solution?

As indicated above, the problem of extraterritorial application of U.S. antitrust law has manifested itself in relation to activities outside the United States of both foreign subsidiaries of U.S. companies and foreign parent companies of U.S. subsidiaries.

The impact of extraterritorial applications of U.S. antitrust laws has made itself felt mainly when foreign companies have been directed by the U.S. courts as to their market behavior, corporate structure, and corporate relationships outside the United States, but cases against foreign subsidiaries or branches of U.S. companies have caused concern. Basically, the resulting problem is the same. Companies operating outside the United States are dictated to as to what is permissible and how they should conduct their business within the territory of another state and within the jurisdiction of that other state.

---

[16] *Grand Jury Subpoena Addressed to First National City Bank*, 396 F. 2nd 897, CCA 2nd (1969).

While the governments of such other states have made protest against many such actions of the United States and have enacted laws to block the intrusion of foreign antitrust legislation, various attempts have been made on the international level to provide for the prevention or resolution of conflicts thus created in antitrust matters through multilateral conventions. All these efforts have failed up to now, basically because antitrust laws are by definition parochial in character. They aim to regulate the national market in a way which is beneficial to the national economy. The same is the case with the integrated communities of the EEC and the European Coal and Steel Community (ECSC). The interests of the various countries with regard to agreements between enterprises and with regard to concentration may be quite different; thus, the interest of exporting countries can be diametrically opposed to the interests of importing countries. In this connection, it is worth noting that U.S. enterprises can be authorized under the Webb-Pomerane Act to conclude export cartels.

It is also a fact, in and by itself, that the concept of competition is not viewed in the same manner in all countries. Competition is not an isolated subject but is a factor in the general economic and political structure of a nation. Like all other aspects of life and law, the concept of competition has evolved in every country under the influence of the character of the people, their traditions, and the economic development of the country.

In the United States, competition is an aim in itself. This aim has been embodied in the law, and the courts accordingly enforce competition. In other countries, the laws of competition are one of the means by which the government protects and influences its national economy. For instance, under Netherlands law, restrictive agreements are not forbidden until the minister decides so, either in individual cases or by category. In Belgium, there is no prohibition of restrictive agreements except as to the primary subsistence needs, but only a prohibition of abuse of a dominant position. Even in the United States there are many laws which exempt certain sectors of the economy from the Sherman Act and thus make inroads on the general principles underlying that law. The reason for this is that it would not be in the interest of the U.S. economy to apply the Sherman Act to those activities. The following U.S. laws can be mentioned here:

Interstate Commerce Act (1887), as amended by the Transportation Act (1920) — (railroad transportation);
Shipping Act (1916), as amended — (shipping);
Communications Act (1934) — (wire and radio communication);
Motor Carriers Act (1935), as amended — (motor carrier transportation);
Civil Aeronautics Act (1938), — (civil airline transportation);
Revenue Act of 1916 — (banking);

Federal Reserve Act, as amended – (banking);

Insurance Regulation Act (1945), as amended – (insurance);

Agricultural Adjustment Act (1933), as amended – (agricultural commodities or processing thereof);

Agriculture, Tobacco-growing, Stockbreeding, Fisheries Packers and Stockyards Act (1921), as amended – (livestock trade);

Capper-Volstead Act (1922) – (agricultural co-operatives);

Perishable Agricultural Commodities Act (1930), as amended – (trade in perishable agriculture commodities);

Fisheries Co-operative Marketing Act (1934) – (fisheries co-operatives);

Poultry Amendment (1935) to the Packers and Stockyards Act – (poultry trade);

State Tobacco Compacts Act (1936) – (tobacco compacts);

Connally Hot Oil Act (1935), as amended – production and marketing of oil);

Interstate Oil Compact Act (1943) – (oil compacts);

Bituminous Coal Act (1937), as amended – (coal industry);

Clayton Act (1914), as amended, and Norris-La Guardia Anti-injunction Act (1932) – (activities of labor unions.)

The above-mentioned laws either exempt a sector of the economy from the application of the antitrust laws or set up an adminstrative, regulatory agency which can authorize restrictive agreements within a particular sector of the economy.

As matters now stand, the U.S. courts endeavor to regulate the market behavior of foreign companies outside the Untied States in situations where the countries in which those foreign companies operate consider this action by the U.S. courts an infringement of their sovereignty. In many instances, they have put up legal barriers to stop the intrusion of U.S. antitrust laws into their economy. From the point of view of promoting European investments in the United States, this is a very unsatisfactory situation.

In discussing the intrusion of U.S. antitrust laws into Canada, the Watkins Report contains recommendations against "the erosion of Canadian sovereignty." The Report recommends:

that Canada undertake initiatives on the national level which will aid in maintaining competition globally. As a first step in promoting international cooperation based on a genuine international consensus Canada should call on all countries to cease extending their particular antitrust law and policy extraterritorially. Positive steps to block the extraterritorial intrusion of the American antitrust laws are recommended below.

●   ●   ●

It is recommended that three specific steps are taken to block the intrusion of foreign antitrust law into Canada: (a) Legislate to prohibit the removal of commercial records and data from business concerns within Federal [Canadian] jurisdiction by reason of a foreign Court order; (b) Use the guiding-principles questionnaire to elicit information on the operational impact of foreign antitrust legislation on the Canadian subsidiaries of foreign corporations; (c) Enact legislation to prohibit Canadian compliance with foreign antitrust orders, decrees, or judgments.[17]

This seems to be a reasonable approach. It goes further than the recommendation addressed to the OECD member states by the OECD Council of Ministers in December, 1967 (Appendix C), because that recommendation does not deal with the problem of extraterritoriality. Rather, it states that the unilateral application of national legislation, in cases where business operations in other countries are involved, raises questions as to the respective spheres of sovereignty of the countries concerned. It further mentions that a closer cooperation between member countries in the form of consultations, exchanges of information, and coordination of efforts on a fully voluntary basis should be encouraged, it being understood that such cooperation should not in any way be construed to affect the legal positions of member countries with regard to such questions of sovereignty, and in particular the extraterritorial application of laws concerning restrictive business practices, as may arise.

Quite aside from the international law question of permissibility of extraterritorial application of national antitrust laws, the practical problem is that this application acts as a deterrent against European investments in the United States, even though there are barriers to the enforcement of extraterritorial application in a numer of countries which have made laws against it. The climate for European investments in the United States would be improved if the U.S. authorities could decide, instead of endeavoring (often without success) to dictate to foreign enterprises how they must behave outside the United States, that individual cases, when they come up, be discussed with the government of the country where the acts would have to be performed, so that—to the extent that the national interests of those governments permit this—they could take U.S. interests into account.

Thus the governments of these countries would be aware of legitimate U.S. interests, and the climate in international antitrust matters would be improved. At the same time, the European enterprises which consider direct investments in the United States would know that their non-U.S. interests would not be intruded upon, except with the affirmative approval of the foreign governments

---

[17]The Watkins Report, *op. cit.,* Chap. V, Sec. 3; Sec. 5. Para. 3.

concerned and in accordance with their own laws. The United States has traditionally opened its doors to other nations and shown its willingness to promote international business relations. Europeans are confident that this same spirit will also prevail in the matter which is the subject of this background chapter and which will be elaborated and discussed in subsequent chapters. In this connection, it is gratifying to note an apparent lessening of extraterritorial applications of the Sherman Act since the modified final judgment in the Swiss watchmakers' case, although there may still be less restraint on the part of the Federal Maritime Commission and other regulatory agencies.

THE LEGAL INSECURITY IN THE SETTING UP OF JOINT VENTURES IN THE UNITED STATES

It has been noted that everybody who performs any act in the United States must do so in conformity with U.S. law, and that every businessman, U.S. or non-U.S. citizen, resident in the United States or abroad is and should be subject to U.S. law regarding his activities in the United States.

Nevertheless, it can happen that the legal hazards inherent in certain rules of U.S. law can have a stronger impact upon the operations of a foreign company than they would have on those of a U.S. company.

In the case of joint ventures between a European company and a U.S. company, as in the case of any joint venture wholly between U.S. companies, the prohibitions of Section 7 of the Clayton Act would apply not only in those cases where there is actual competition which may be substantially lessened but also where the courts may find that the relevant competition is no more than potential, that is, where there is a reasonable probability that any one of the companies participating in the joint venture would have entered the market alone with the other remaining a significant, potential competitor.[18] However, the gravity of the problem is not that a joint venture can be prohibited from its inception. The difficulties arise specifically when a joint venture between a European company and a U.S. company is attacked after it has been in operation for a number of years.

By way of example, mention could be made of the consent decree which involved Monsanto, Mobay, and Bayer companies.[19] This consent decree required a U.S. company (Monsanto) to sell all of its interests in a U.S. joint venture (Mobay) to the other shareholder (Bayer). The joint venture had been

---

[18] *United States v. Penn-Olin Chem. Co.,* 217 F. Supp. 110 D. Del. (1963); 378 U.S. 158 (1964); 246 F. Supp. 917 (1965); 387 U.S. 906 (1967).

[19] *United States v. Monsanto Co., Farbenfabriken Bayer AG, and Mobay Chemical Co.,* CCH 1967 Trade Cases, Par. 72,001 W.D. Pa. (1967).

established by Monsanto and Bayer in 1954 for the production and sale if isocyanates and other products used in the manufacture of polyurethane products. It was very successful, and by 1962, its eighth year of operation, it had acquired 50 per cent of the U.S. market. In 1967, however, Monsanto was obliged by the consent decree to give up its interest in the joint venture. Apparently this was required because Monsanto had substantially terminated its own production and sale of isocyanates in the United States, and Bayer had not exported any substantive quantity of isocyanates to U.S. companies other than Mobay.

These two cases evidence the legal difficulties and risks involved in this country. The more successful such a venture may be, the greater the risk that at a future date it will draw the attention of the Department of Justice, which may then decide to invoke Section 7 against its continued operation. Even though the combined market share at the outset might have been sufficiently small to make the venture reasonably secure against attack under Section 7, its market share may have grown many years later (as with Mobay) to the extent that the combination might then be vulnerable. In the words of Professor Jules Backman:

> Who is a potential competitor? Because of the nature of our competitive economy, he or they cannot always be identified in advance. Is it any company which has the ability to surmount existing barriers to entry such as capital requirements, technological know-how, sales contracts among potential customers, patents, etc.? If potential is to be defined so broadly, then practically every chemical company—and many companies in other industries which use chemical processes—is a potential competitor for most products. This would be particularly true when "turnkey" plants can be acquired. However, such a broad definition of "potential" would not be too meaningful. In realistic terms, the field usually is much narrower. The number of potential competitors changes as economic conditions change.[20]

The fact that the legal status of an acquisition can change during the years was confirmed by Assistant Attorney General Edwin M. Zimmerman at a hearing on August 30, 1966, before the U.S. Senate Sub-Committee on Antitrust and Monopoly, when, talking about mergers and acquisitions, he stressed that

---

[20] Jules Backman, "Joint Ventures in the Light of Recent Antitrust Developments: Joint Ventures in the Chemical Industry," *The Antitrust Bulletin*, Vol. X, No. 1 (January–April, 1965), p. 12.

"merger cases never close."[21]

In addition to the foregoing, legal insecurity for the European investor is increased because it is extremely difficult for him to learn with any reasonable degree of certainty what the policy of the U.S. law enforcement authorities might be from time to time with regard to joint ventures. Thus, one leading expert in this country said:

> Unfortunately there is today no coherent enforcement policy at the Antitrust Division which can be discerned by the outside observer. Businessmen interested in combination mergers or joint ventures must engage in what is little more than a lottery. It is well known that the Antitrust Division does not have sufficient funds or personnel resources to apply the laws equally to all combinations of this kind. While much has been made of the Division's attack on mergers, for example, it is significant that it has actually proceeded against only 49 mergers out of a total of 4,960 recorded in the past four fiscal Government years. Many mergers like those attacked went scot-free. One can confidently expect that a similar condition will exist as to joint ventures. Some joint ventures, both past and present, will be attacked, while many similar joint ventures involving unquestionably the same basic factual situations will go unchallenged.
>
> Since the Antitrust Division is purely an enforcement agency, this condition may not be wholly avoidable, given the enormous diversity and complexity of American business. It is, however, a condition which has been unnecessarily aggravated by the failure of the Antitrust Division to maintain a coherent enforcement policy. Too often the individual businessman is left to make decisions for his business without knowing whether his competitors' status is secure or whether his own company will be attacked if he seeks to emulate them.[22]

European companies often feel that they cannot penetrate into the U.S. market by themselves. To be able to do so, they may decide to join their efforts with a U.S. company, and they may choose the form of a joint venture. If, after

[21]U.S. Senate, *International Aspects of Antitrust*, Committee on the Judiciary, 89th Cong., 2nd Sess., August 30, 1966, p. 498.

[22]Gerhard A. Gesell, "Joint Ventures in the Light of Recent Antitrust Developments: Joint Ventures and the Prosecutor," *The Antitrust Bulletin,* Vol. X, No. 1 (January–April, 1965), pp. 34-35.

several years of operation, the European company should be obliged to sell its share in the joint company to its U.S. partner, all its endeavors to penetrate the U.S. market might have become fruitless. If, on the other hand, the U.S. partner should be required to step out of the joint venture, the European partner would be deprived of the cooperation of the U.S. enterprise which it might need to maintain itself on the U.S. market. Admittedly, there may be cases where the European company, after having cooperated for some time with its U.S. partner, would have become able to hold its position alone. There may also be cases where the opposite were true, and where the European company alone would not be able to survive on the U.S. market. In any case, there are serious risks for the European investor who selects the form of a joint venture that at some moment the Department of Justice might decide should no longer be maintained.

Going back to an earlier theme of this chapter, it might be noted here that divorcement proceedings under U.S. law are not limited to joint ventures established within the territory of the United States. In the ICI case described above, the U.S. court decided that the joint interests of Du Pont and ICI in Argentina, Brazil, and Canada had to be terminated by either Du Pont or ICI disposing of its share in the joint enterprises.

Admittedly, this drastic remedy was resorted to as part of the over-all injunction against agreements to divide world markets. However, it is not clear to the European partner of a joint enterprise with a U.S. company how far U.S. injunctions against combinations which involved foreign interests might reach. In view of the ICI and other cases, if a U.S. court should conclude that a combination in the United States or elsewhere were unlawful, it could order a dissolution even as to joint companies abroad, particularly where it might conclude that foreign combinations had "effects" on the foreign commerce of the United States.

There is still another aspect which cannot but worry European investors. It has been shown that a foreign company making a direct investment in the United States might become subject to the jurisdiction of the U.S. courts as to its foreign activities. These might include mergers and other acquisitions abroad. The Clayton Act as well as the Sherman Act has been applied extraterritorially, and there is the risk that acquisitions abroad by foreign companies might be attacked, just as in the case of acquisitions abroad by U.S. companies.[23] From the testimony of Assistant Attorney General Zimmerman at the hearing mentioned above, it appears that Section 7 of the Clayton Act is wide enough to be applied to mergers abroad, even as between two non-U.S. companies, if there is substantial restraint of U.S. commerce resulting from the merger. He said:

---

[23]Note the proposed acquisition by Gillette of the German enterprise Bruan: *United States v. Gillette Co,,* CCH Trade Reg. Rep. par. 45,068, D. Mass. (1968).

In the usual case of a merger or joint venture abroad, the primary impact would appear to be in the foreign country where the arrangement takes place. However, in some instances, there may also be sufficient impact on U.S. foreign trade for the Department to bring suit . . . In any case where there appears to be a substantial restraint of U.S. trade resulting from the merger, we will take appropriate action under the antitrust laws.[24]

U.S. SECURITIES EXCHANGE LEGISLATION AND REGULATIONS ISSUED THEREUNDER

We have not mentioned problems confronting European direct investments in the United States. These problems have been due to a large extent to the fact that the U.S. antitrust enforcement authorities have in the past failed to give proper recognition to the differences between U.S. and foreign concepts in the matter of economic competition. Fortunately, this is not the general picture, and to conclude this chapter it seems opportune to show that it is possible to take into account the legitimate interests of foreign companies without prejudice to the national interest.

In this connection, it ought to be mentioned that, in the matter of the U.S. securities legislation, the SEC has shown its willingness to find ways and means which, on the one hand, are consistent with the protection of investors in the United States, but, on the other hand, also take into account the legitimate standpoint of foreign companies that the effect of U.S. legislation should not be extended to foreign companies which have virtually no active connection whatsoever with the United States.

The Securities Exchange Act of 1934 was amended in 1964, in order to extend the registration requirements under the act to issuers whose securities are traded on the over-the-counter market in the United States, provided that the company concerned has assets in excess of $1 million and such securities are held by 500 or more persons. The Congressional history of the 1964 amendments makes it clear that Congress intended the said requirements also to apply to foreign issuers of such securities. However, power was given to the SES to grant exemption to any foreign issuer if the SES found that such exemption were in the public interest and consistent with the protection of investors.

After the above-mentioned amendment was incorporated in the act, the SES temporarily exempted all foreign companies whose securities were traded

---

[24]U.S. Senate, *International Aspects of Antitrust, op, cit.,* p. 491.

over the counter from the requirement to register, pending its consideration of possible rules and regulations. Some time thereafter, the SES proposed rules which would exempt all such foreign companies having less than 300 shareholders resident in the United States. Foreign companies having more than 300 shareholders were divided basically in two categories, North American foreign companies and other foreign companies. The first category would have to comply with all the regulations of the Securities and Exchange Act, including those relating to insider trading and proxy solicitation. The other companies would have to furnish certain information but would be exempted in principle from the insider trading and proxy solicitation provisions.

The rules originally proposed by the SES created strong objections from abroad, including objections from the governments of Canada and Great Britain. The rules finally adopted by the SES in April, 1967, provided, although in principle foreign issuers having more than 300 shareholders resident in the United States were required to register with the SES, that they could obtain an exemption from this requirement if they or an official of their government furnished voluntarily to the commission substantially the same information as they (1) would have to make public pursuant to the laws of the country of their incorporation, (2) would have to file with a foreign stock exchange on which their securities were traded and which was made public by such exchanges, or (3) would have distributed to their security holders. In addition, the distinction between foreign North American and other foreign companies was dropped entirely and thereby also the requirement for foreign North American companies whose securities were not listed on a U.S. stock exchange and who had not actively sought the capital market in the United States to comply with the proxy solicitation rules and insider trading provisions.

CHAPTER 4

U.S. ANTITRUST POLICY AND DIRECT FOREIGN INVESTMENT

Richard W. McLaren

INTRODUCTION

Antitrust laws in the United States have the task of maintaining a competitive economy, free from unduly restrictive practices or market domination. In a period when growing concentration of economic power within the United States is becoming a matter of increasing concern, the introduction of new sources of competition from abroad would make that task considerably easier.

As is well known, the procompetitive philosophy behind U.S. antitrust laws has been given a great deal of credit for the country's vigorous, imaginative, and flexible business spirit. The economic rationale and the fruits of competition certainly need not be reviewed here; indeed, since World War II many other nations have adopted or strengthened their antitrust laws.

U.S. ANTITRUST POLICY AND THE FOREIGN INVESTOR

What does antitrust policy mean to the foreign businessman who is thinking about investing in the U.S. market? First, it means that he is more than welcome. New products, new technology, new competition can only be a plus for the American economy. Second, it means that he is assured of a fair chance to compete for a share of the market. Exclusionary or discriminatory business practices directed at foreign firms will be given no better treatment at the Antitrust Division or the Federal Trade Commission than those in which a U.S. firm is the victim. And third, it means that the United States is quite serious about antitrust enforcement and has a duty to enforce the law with an even hand. Like other nations, it has a responsibility to prevent deliberate violations of the law. In other words, in a very important sense antitrust laws in the United States provide a distinct advantage to the foreign company doing business there.

The Historical Perspective

In the past, relatively few foreign companies have run into difficulties with U.S. antitrust law in connection with their direct investments there. The Mobay case involving Monsanto and Bayer, which was mentioned in Chapter 3, apparently caused a good deal of discussion in Europe, but it should cause no great concern as to investment in the United States. The facts of the case are somewhat complex, but the essential principles are simple.

The complaint in the Mobay case charged that a joint venture in the United States between Monsanto and Bayer of Germany violated Section 1 of the Sherman Act. Joint ventures are not necessarily illegal under U.S. law. This one, however, was between two of the world's largest chemical companies in an important new chemical product, isocyanates—a raw material for plastic foam used, for example, as a lightweight lining for clothes. The complaint charged that the companies were actual as well as potential competitors in the U.S. market. By the time of the suit, they had, in their joint venture, 50 per cent of the market. Accordingly, it is not surprising that this joint venture received antitrust attention.

The lesson from this case is clear. If one needs a U.S. partner (it is not clear that Bayer did), and if one is considering a large U.S. company in the same industry, it is wise to seek clearance from the U.S. Department of Justice or the Federal Trade Commission. The Mobay case should certainly not discourage foreign companies from direct investment in the U.S. market. The outcome of the case, by the way, was a consent decree under which the German company got the entire U.S. business financed, as we understand, by a loan from a New York bank.

The present results of the recent case attacking the Atlantic Richfield-Sinclair merger also indicate that the U.S. Department of Justice does not oppose direct investment by foreign companies. Moreover, it shows that an acquisition even by a large foreign company of a large U.S. company in the same industry is not always barred. When Sinclair proposed selling its Atlantic Coast properties to British Petroleum (BP) as an alternative to Atlantic Richfield and it appeared that British Petroleum—not then in the U.S. market—would be a new and positive competitive force in that market, this acquisition was not opposed. Perhaps the very substantial success in the United States of a well-known oil company from a European country may have stimulated BP's interest in entering the U.S. market.

We have mentioned the availability of clearance procedures by the Department of Justice and the Federal Trade Commission (FTC). These are particularly applicable to mergers and joint ventures in which the antitrust agency normally will, itself, wish to make a prompt decision on a possible suit when the matter is called to its attention. The Justice Department has what is termed a "business review procedure." After reviewing a proposed merger or other action or agreement (presented in writing together with any additional requested information), the Justice Department will set forth its litigation intentions in the specific instance. The Federal Trade Commission has a Bureau of Advisory Opinions, which renders the same type of advice. (We may say, in passing, that the Justice Department and the FTC have a close liaison on enforcement matters to avoid duplication of action on matters over which both have jurisdiction.) These clearance procedures are available to foreign as well as U.S. companies. There is always an open door to businessmen and their lawyers for discussion of their problems.

We are certain at this point that many readers are still asking: "Granted that vigorous antitrust enforcement may be highly desirable for the United States, *why* does the United States insist on trying to force antitrust on the rest of the world by extraterritorial application of U.S. law?"

In the first place, the charges of extraterritorial enforcement have always seemed to us quite exaggerated.

It is certainly true that, if the "effects" theory were carried to its logical extreme, U.S. courts might assert jurisdiction over some very minor activities of foreign citizens carried out in a country where those activities were perfectly legal, as long as there were an *effect* upon U.S. domestic or foreign commerce that was condemned by U.S. law. But while the limits, if any, of the so-called effects theory of legislative jurisdiction are fertile ground for abstract discussion (and, lest we forget, Judge Learned Hand in the famous Alcoa case clearly recognized that international law places limitations on how far the exercise of jurisdiction may be carried), we can hardly think that today the *concept* is open to serious question. Many U.S. laws—not just the antitrust laws—condemn certain activities regardless of where they physically take place or of the nationality of those who engage in them. The American Law Institute, in its Restatement of the Foreign Relations Law of the United States, has concluded that a nation may properly assert jurisdiction over acts of both nationals and aliens abroad which have effects within that country.

Moreover, the "effects" basis of jurisdiction is just as popular in other countries, even with respect to their antitrust legislation. The Federal Republic of Germany and Austria, for example, expressly extend their laws to include restrictive business practices abroad having "effects" within their territory. The EEC commission has indicated that it would similarly construe Article 85 of the Rome Treaty, and the Canadian Restrictive Trade Practices Commission has so interpreted Canadian law. To do otherwise and make enforcement turn on nationality or physical events would open the door to the possibility of widespread evasion and abuse. In addition to "tax havens" and "shipping havens" that now exist, there would be countries that would set themselves up as "antitrust havens." An island in the Caribbean or a city in Latin America with no antitrust law (or, better yet, a law *requiring* cooperation among businesses) would quickly become the number one convention center in the Western Hemisphere.

As a corollary to the line of reasoning described above, some critics insist that application of U.S. law to foreign trade as well as to domestic trade unjustifiably encroaches upon the sovereignty of other nations. Assuming that the same criticism would be made of a foreign country that attempted to regulate the same international trade, and carrying this to its logical conclusion, international trade (which necessarily involves the economic interests of two or more nations) could be regulated by no one, and private interest would be free to do as they please in this never-never land. It seems to us that to state the proposition is to refute it.

This does not mean, of course, that there have not been legitimate differences of opinion in specific cases brought in this area. Probably because such cases as ICI-British Nylon Spinners are so rare, they receive more than their share of attention. (See Chapter 3.) The statutes that prohibit the production of business records pursuant to a foreign court order also fall in this category. But these cases not only point out the problem, they indicate the solution as well. Because international trade by definition involves the interests of two or more nations, it is only at the governmental level that these problems can be handled without leaving an unregulated "enforcement gap." We are pleased to say that preliminary efforts at intergovernmental understanding in this area have been under way for several years, both on a bilateral and a multilateral basis. We are optimistic with regard to the results.

SUMMARY

In closing this chapter, let us emphasize that U.S. antitrust legislation does not concern itself with the activities of non-U.S. companies as they affect the citizens or economies of other countries.[1] While those in the United States are, of course, interested in continued prosperity and economic freedom everywhere, they recognize that every nation has the right to decide for itself the path it will take. In its choice of a competitive system enforced by law, the United States has the company of many nations. Because this sytem has been extremely successful here, those who do invest in the United States share a community of interest in keeping a free economy.

---

[1]It is noteworthy that most of the decrees cited in Chapter 3 by Mr. Ellis as horrible examples of extraterritoriality involved U.S. and foreign companies in cartel situations—which are now also illegal under various foreign laws.

5

U.S. DIRECT INVESTMENT IN EUROPE

Rainer Hellmann

INTRODUCTION

Since the 1950's, U.S. direct investments have had an important and beneficial influence on the economies of Western European countries. These effects are not analyzed in this chapter, which is limited to certain developments during the period of U.S. capital export controls, notably how the controls have affected the forms of direct investment and how these developments were appraised in Western Europe. The author has of necessity neglected many other relevant factors. His conclusions are based upon interviews and personal evaluation of available data. They cannot be proved by statistics and are open to discussion.

EFFECT OF U.S. CAPITAL EXPORT CONTROL, 1965—69

The years 1965 to 1969 have been a period of particular challenge to U.S. investment in Western Europe. From 1965 to 1967, the U.S. Government restricted capital exports for direct investment by guidelines, and, since January 1, 1968, by a mandatory program. Both restraints sought to limit capital outflow, especially to Western Europe. These programs confronted U.S. companies and European recipient nations with the question of whether U.S. investment in Western Europe would continue as before. Further, U.S. companies had to decide whether to continue their European investment as it could no longer be financed in the customary ways.

The European recipient countries had to decide whether they should continue to tolerate, or favor, new foreign-owned industry in their territory if the investment were financed only to a very limited extent by U.S. capital. Even in the years 1962 to 1965, only an average of 20 per cent of U.S. direct investment in Western Europe was financed by funds from the United States, while more than 30 per cent was financed abroad, the remaining 50 per cent being divided almost equally between retained earnings and depreciation.

The answer to these questions was a clear "yes" on both sides of the Atlantic. Annoying as all restrictions are, the two programs, above all the mandatory one have had the advantage of making both Europeans and Americans think more deeply about foreign investment. On both sides of the Atlantic, new ways were found to attain investment objectives.

Plant and equipment expenditures of U.S. companies in Western Europe rose from $2.18 billion in 1964, the last year before restrictions, to $3.64 billion in 1967. The corresponding sums for 1968 and 1969 are estimated at roughly $3.8 billion each. In the Common Market alone, U.S. plant and equipment expenditures almost doubled from $1.1 billion in 1964 to $2.04 in 1967 and will probably remain about the same in 1968 and 1969 if current estimates prove correct.

The voluntary guidelines could not curb the soaring investment in Western Europe. As of 1968, the steeply rising investment trend seems to flatten out at a very high yearly level of new plant and equipment expenditures. There is no evidence that the flattening of the trend is due solely to the mandatory program. It seems rather that other factors—particularly the 1968 boom in the United States—have influenced this development.

Under the present economic conditions in the United States and Europe, a sudden and major increase in the U.S. direct investment in Western Europe seems unlikely, even if the mandatory program were relaxed or abandoned. In the future, a larger proportion of U.S. investment in Europe will probably be financed outside the United States, even without any restraint on exports of capital. The Euro-market will continue to play an important role in financing it. These developments make European countries more sensitive to problems connected with some forms of U.S. direct investment and to the exercise of U.S. Government influence on it.

DIVERSIFICATION OF U.S. INVESTMENT
IN EUROPE

By Area

U.S. investment in Western Europe has become more diversified since the mid–1960's, both geographically and in distribution by industries. The book value of U.S. investment in three of the larger European countries—the United

Kingdom, France, and Italy—increased only by about one third from 1964 to 1967. Among the larger European countries, only West Germany registered an important increase in book value from $2.1 billion in 1964 to $3.5 billion at the end of 1967. In smaller European countries, the value of U.S. investment rose as fast or faster than in Germany, particularly in Spain, Belgium, the Netherlands, and Switzerland. U.S. investment has also increased rapidly in the Scandinavian countries. Greece and Austria have been favored by U.S. direct investment since the second half of 1967. Austria may become a favorite location for U.S. companies wanting to enter Eastern European markets.

The importance of U.S. investment varies from marginal to deeply significant among different European countries. In the Scandanavian countries, plant and equipment expenditures of U.S.-owned companies are still marginal, with 1 per cent to 3 per cent of the total investment flow of the manufacturing industries. In Germany and Italy, this rate has gone up from 6 per cent to 9 per cent, and in France, from 4 to 6 per cent. In Great Britain, the large base of U.S. investment assures a relatively constant yearly rate of some 15 per cent. In the Netherlands, the U.S. investment share has risen in a few years from 8 to 15 per cent, and in Belgium, from 6 to almost 20 per cent in 1967, alone. In Greece, an even steeper rise may be going on now. Such a steeply rising share makes U.S. investment in these countries an almost vital element for their economic expansion. As this flow of expenditures on plants and equipment is very high compared to the U.S. investment base in these countries, they rely heavily on its continuity. They are, therefore, particularly concerned about the possibility of further U.S. restrictions being imposed without warning.

By Industry

The largest investment in Western Europe has been in the oil, chemical, transportation equipment, metals, machinery, electrical, and food industries. They continue to be the most important industries for U.S. investment, but their share is decreasing. Other industries are becoming more attractive. A few years ago, glass, paper, and pharmaceuticals began to attract significant investment; now textiles, ceramics, recreation, and especially services are also included. From 1963 to 1967, takeover bids by U.S. companies in the automobile and oil industries brought their share of the market to more than 30 per cent. However, the increase seems to have stopped. European chemical companies are now investing as fast as their U.S. competitors in Europe. The very large share of U.S. companies in the computer industry in Europe will probably decrease slowly as European companies are making great efforts to catch up.

On the other hand, the stake in U.S. hotels, banking, brokerage, and publicity agencies is increasing rapidly. They first came to Europe to serve the

U.S. manufacturing industry, but today their U.S. clients in many cases account for only 10 to 20 per cent of their business. The development of the Euro-market has proved particularly attractive for U.S. banking.

The book value of U.S. investment in the service industries may not be very large, as capital is often needed only for office space and staff. Nevertheless, U.S. investment in this "third sector" has an important influence on European economic and public life in general, an influence which, moreover, is more direct than the influence of investment in the oil or manufacturing industries. In fact, U.S. investment in recent years—and not only in the services—has been determined to an important extent by new ideas and new ways of presentation.

New ideas and services offered by U.S. companies are taken up rapidly by European competitors if the consumer accepts and wants them. Patent law has little or no restrictive effect in the services as it does in manufacturing. The direct effect of U.S. investment on European productivity may therefore become evident sooner than in previous periods.

CRITERIA FOR THE WELCOME OF
U.S. INVESTMENT IN EUROPE

The four years of capital-export restrictions on direct investment have proved that U.S. investment in the form of new plants and equipment is welcome in Europe even without a dollar inflow. On the other hand, growing resistance against takeovers of large European companies by U.S. firms needs further analysis.

New Investment

According to John H. Dunning of the University of Reading, foreign investment represents "a package deal comprised of three ingredients: (1) enterpreneurship, that elusive and ill-defined fourth factor of production; (2) expertise, technological and managerial; and (3) money capital."

During the mid-1960's, Europe has been no longer in search of money capital. The long-continued deficit in the U.S. balance of payments helped to bring the Euro-capital market into existence. This market has proved capable of financing not only the needs of U.S. investors in Europe, but of more and more large, private, and state-owned European companies. Some U.S. companies have even financed their expansion or takeovers in the United States by borrowing on the Euro-market.

What Europe still needs is the combination of entrepreneurship and technological expertise, those "new combinations," detected some decades ago by Joseph Schumpeter as the sources of profit, growth, and economic development. U.S. investors have secured them, thus engaging themselves in irreversible, new, direct investment in Western Europe and demonstrating their confidence in the European situation and its possibilities.

The welcome for U.S. investors has grown warmer, even in France. The period during which the French Government sought to limit U.S. investment by selective methods reached its peak in 1963-64. Now even the French Government has become interested in U.S. investors seeking the best location. A new U.S. automobile equipment plant was actively sought by the French Government, which was unhappy when other U.S. investors chose to invest outside its borders. In fact, this may mean that French workers earn their living in a U.S. plant across the border which is paying its taxes to a neighboring country. There have been French among the European missions which have visited several U.S. states in order to interest U.S. investment in specific regions.

Belgium, a country which has always welcomed new U.S. investment, asked its semiofficial investment bank in 1968 to lend U.S. investors up to 100 per cent of the sums needed to maintain a high level of U.S. investment flow despite the mandatory restrictions.

The subsidies paid directly and indirectly by European states, regions, and local authorities to encourage investment—particularly all U.S. investment—have not diminished but increased since 1965. The Common Market Commission has warned that this competition for more and more advantageous investment conditions is dangerous for the truly underdeveloped regions in the Common Market, e.g., for Southern Italy. The commission has sought, so far unsuccessfully, to limit these artificial incentives.

It is important to keep in mind the different motivations for the United States and Europe today to encourage reciprocal foreign investment. The United States tries to attract foreign portfolio and direct investors in order to improve its balance of payments. The European incentives are given to fill a gap in risk-taking direct investment in technologically advanced industries. If necessary, European countries are ready to finance this investment on their own capital markets.

Takeovers

The warm welcome for new U.S. investment in Europe—with or without dollars—was never extended to the acquisition of existing European enterprise by U.S. companies. Not only the French Government but also governments known for their liberal position—Belgium or West Germany—have taken direct or indirect steps to prevent takeovers. Even in Switzerland and Austria, takeover projects have been abandoned in response to adverse public opinion.

In 1967, the German Government blocked U.S. efforts and in 1969, French efforts to obtain a minority participation in the German oil company, Aral. In November, 1967, when the Petrofina Oil Company became the object of foreign interest, the Belgian Government issued a regulation which submits takeover of Belgian companies by foreigners to previous government authorization. A takeover bid for Jeumont, a producer of electrical equipment, by a U.S. company was still being blocked by the French Government in 1969.

The real importance of takeovers in the framework of direct investment is difficult to assess. Statistics—even those of the U.S. Department of Commerce—are general and unspecific. According to them, acquisition of existing Western European enterprises by U.S. companies has had a 10 to 12 per cent share in total U.S. investment in Europe in recent years. In any event, the psychological effect of takeovers on goodwill toward foreign direct investment in general is more important than their real importance. A conscious distinction between the two methods of direct investment is rarely made.

New plant and equipment investment brings new employment, new incentives for the use of subcontractors, new technology, and more competition to a country or region. This is undoubtedly profitable unless there is already full employment or an overcapacity in the specific industry.

On the other hand, a takeover represents change in an existing situation, and changes into uncertainty are rarely welcomed. Whether the change will be profitable or not cannot be told beforehand, but it is known from the start that control over a company built up by European enterprise is passing to the other side of the Atlantic. Local influence on the plant may therefore diminish.

Many acquisitions which have been bitterly contested at the time of the takeover have proved highly beneficial for the enterprise, the workers, and the whole region. In other cases, the staff, the workers, and the plant could not fit into the new organization directed by the U.S. parent. Traditions were too strong or the change too abrupt. These affiliates were shaken by labor conflicts which in some cases lasted for years.

Governments therefore sometimes work out conditions under which they agree to a specific takeover, thus trying to assure employment for the workers and the staff and to guarantee the maintenance of the plant in the region or the country. To the extent that security of employment and of social standards are guaranteed, such conditions may be helpful. On the other hand, it would be unrealistic to try to avoid any change. In international foreign investment, one must accept the right of the parent company to take vital policy and investment decisions centrally. Conditions which frustrate global strategies of the parent company are worse than foregoing a takeover.

The local reaction to takeovers by foreign companies depends on many factors which are still insufficiently analyzed. The size of the company, the foreign capital already invested in the industry, and the character of the industry are relevant criteria. Between 1962 and 1967, some important acquisitions in such basic or national prestige industries as automobiles, oil, and computers were often discussed in Europe for months before approval. In recent years, it has become increasingly difficult to buy European companies worth more than $50 million. An acquisition similar to that by British Petroleum in the United States—$400 million—would no longer be imaginable in Western Europe.

U.S. companies, seeking to catch up with larger U.S. competitors, often 'prefer the quicker way of new acquisition rather than making a new investment which has a longer maturing period. Takeovers in Europe were most frequent in industries with two or three major U.S. competitors. In the automobile, electrical equipment, and computer industries, U.S. companies holding the second or third position in the U.S. market have generally been the most active in European acquisitions. If a U.S. company with the largest share in the U.S. market is acquiring European companies, as for instance in the textile industry, it may be trying to avoid the effects of U.S. antitrust legislation. In order not to increase its U.S. market share, the company is investing part of its profits in the purchase of European companies. However, even this is no safe escape from U.S. antitrust legislation, as the Gillette-Braun case proves.

There are specific reasons why many European companies are for sale and why their owners often prefer a U.S. to a European offer. Reasons why European owners want to sell companies or parts of companies include the three following items: (1) the fear, in the long run, that medium-sized companies can survive international competition only if they profit from the research and technological capacities and the international sales and service systems of a large company operating on a multinational scale; (2) the necessity to sell part of an enterprise in order to specialize and to operate on a multinational scale in the remaining sector of activity. (An important European family enterprise sold its office-machinery department in order to invest internationally in the radio and television branch. Such a policy is the direct opposite of the policy practiced by U.S. conglomerates.); and (3) the fact that many European companies are in the hands of one family which cannot provide for continuity in management. (In recent years many German companies have sold out because the owners, in their sixties, wanted to ensure efficient management for their firm).

Even when competing with European companies, U.S. corporations succeed more easily in acquisitions as they are ready to pay a higher price and to pay it immediately. U.S. companies can generally get more plant in Europe than they could buy in the United States for the same dollar amount. If they cannot pay the sum from profits or depreciation out of their existing foreign plant, they are ready to pay the high interest rates for a straight loan in the Euro-capital market or to issue bonds convertible into their own stock, thus paying a lower interest rate. The underrated stock prices on most of the European stock exchanges are specially attractive for U.S. companies. In the past years, first German, then French and Italian, and now Belgian companies seem particularly attractive to U.S. investors.

European companies have not had much experience with takeover bids. In France, the public takeover bid of the smaller BSN glass producer for the traditional S. Gobain Company was considered revolutionary. European companies are rarely in a financial position to act quickly and efficiently on their own. When European companies were able to compete successfully with a U.S. corporation in a takeover issue, they were often helped by local banks.

Joint Ventures

Joint ventures are generally considered to be a particularly welcome form of investment by European governments. In fact, many joint ventures have proved highly profitable for both partners. The successful joint ventures were set up generally by partners in equally strong but complementary positions. It is not necessary that both partners be of the same size, but they should bring equally interesting assets for the joint venture in such a way that none of them could run the company alone.

Joint ventures in which the partners are not sufficiently complementary generally remain unstable. If one company is in a weaker position, its part in the joint venture is often acquired by the stronger partner, who then runs the company alone. This has happened rather frequently in joint ventures for which the European partner was insufficiently prepared.

Joint ventures between equally strong partners may also be unstable when each parent company wants to influence directly the policy of the common affiliate. Joint ventures need one center of decision, which should be the board of the joint venture itself. This means autonomy from both parent companies and does not necessarily fit into the picture of a centrally directed corporation acting on a multinational scale.

The joint venture is an interesting form of international investment which can solve specific production and investment problems in specific industries. It is the only possible form of international investment in countries excluding fully owned foreign investment. But it is not the model for general foreign investment in a world free of restrictions.

GOVERNMENT INTERFERENCE

The decision to admit or exclude foreign direct investment is a political decision which every country takes in the light of its own political, social, and economic structure and evolution. The Japanese and Yugoslavian examples prove that the attitude can change in an evolving situation.

Countries open for incoming and outflowing foreign investments do not automatically renounce influence on these investments. The resulting government interference is always resented as an obstacle to the central decision-making capacity of corporations operating on a multinational scale. The governments of the host countries must be aware that the conditions they impose on new foreign investment—and more frequently on takeovers—are restricting global strategies, which are the major advantage of this type of corporation. The intervention may be useful and necessary to achieve social and local aims, but it may also impede the development of the local subsidiary in the international framework assigned to it by the parent corporation. Many of the conditions drafted when the concession for a foreign investment or an acquisition is granted fall into oblivion after two or three years because facts are stronger than regulations.

Also government intervention by the capital exporting countries generates problems for the recipient countries and for the local subsidiaries. Unfortunately, U.S. Government intervention has become more frequent and generated more conflicts in recent years. It is no longer the application of the U.S. tax system on the profits of foreign subsidiaries which generates tensions. It is the extraterritorial application of the antitrust legislation, the Trading with the Enemy Act, and the mandatory Foreign Direct Investment Program, mainly the compulsory repatriation of the 1968 earnings of foreign affiliates to the United States.

Even when governments and countries are ready to recognize the right of foreign corporations to take vital policy and investment decisions centrally, they will not necessarily accept the intervention of the foreign government or legislation, even if this intervention is exercised only upon the U.S. capital owner.

U.S. Government intervention may be detrimental to the "European goodwill" which every U.S. subsidiary tries to build up. Such intervention may disturb the goal strategy of the parent company in a similar way to that of the local government. Compulsory repatriation of earnings is a significant example. In the case of a joint venture, the U.S. partner had to inform his European associate that, due to U.S. Government regulations, he was not free to decide upon the reinvestment of the 1968 earnings of his capital share.

There is hope that the Foreign Direct Investment Program and even some of the export regulations to Communist countries are temporary measures. But antitrust legislation is due to last.

Europeans are aware of the fact that the U.S. Government and Congress must prevent U.S. citizens and companies from violating U.S. legislation via foreign investment. Negotiations between the United States and Europe on foreign investment problems would be easier if Europe could speak with one voice and if the legislation of the European countries were sufficiently harmonized. For the U.S. Government, it must seem a hopeless attempt to negotiate different treaties with each European country, treaties which can never by applied uniformly and which always present loopholes.

The extraterritorial application of U.S. legislation in Europe will probably only be abandoned when Europe has its own legislation on antitrust, foreign trade, and investment, or when an international agreement on these matters has been reached. In the meantime, it would be in the interest of the United States, as the most important foreign investor, to restrict to a minimum the extraterritorial application of its legislation in Europe.

CHAPTER **6** FOREIGN
DIRECT
INVESTMENT
IN CANADA

Thomas L. Powrie

INTRODUCTION

This chapter covers four topics: first, the amount of foreign direct investment in Canada; second, the economic performance of foreign-owned firms; third, the application of foreign laws and policy directives to Canadian subsidiaries of foreign firms; and fourth, the effect on domestic monetary and fiscal policy tools of the increased international mobility of capital that foreign direct investment encourages.

Canada relies on foreign capital to finance from one fifth to two fifths of her capital formation, and over half of this foreign capital is new, direct investments or ploughed-back earnings of existing subsidiaries. The United States owns four fifths of the foreign direct investments in Canada; almost all the rest is owned in the United Kingdom and Continental Europe. Much of the investment is in export-oriented industries based on natural resources, but manufacturing and other activities for the domestic market also contain large amounts of it.

The large proportion of foreign ownership and control in certain important sectors of the economy has been discussed at great length in Canada.[1] It is

---

[1] The discussion in Canada has been mainly about the question: "Direct investment or no direct investment?" There has been relatively little analysis of such other alternatives as joint ventures, purchase of patent rights, recruitment of foreign executives for Canadian firms, and so on.

generally agreed that foreign-owned firms make an important contribution to Canadian economic growth through their capital, management skills, advanced technology, and access to export markets, and that the benefits are reasonably widely diffused among Canadian consumers, workers, and taxpayers. Therefore, the discussion in Canada (and in this chapter) takes it for granted that foreign investment is worth having, and concentrates on the question of how to widen the margin between its benefits and its costs.[2]

One question discussed is the economic performance of foreign-owned firms. Does the fact that a firm is owned by foreigners reduce or increase the contributions that it makes to the Canadian economy? There are various particular differences of performance between foreign and domestically owned firms. However, the main conclusion is that the over-all environment created by government policy, including policy toward external trade, is the primary source of problems that exist in the performance of foreign and domestically owned firms alike. Foreign ownership per se does not, in general, reduce a firm's contribution to the Canadian economy.

Then there is the question of extraterritoriality, that is, the extraterritorial extension of other countres' jurisdictions into Canada through the application of their laws and policy directives to the Canadian subsidiaries of foreign firms. This is a difficult issue. A subsidiary firm in a host country may be subject to the laws of its parent's country because it is controlled by the parent who is subject to those laws. At the same time, the host country would prefer that all firms operating in its territory be subject only to its own laws. It appears that various Canadian-U.S. compromises and agreements have overcome the main economic problems that this dilemma has created for Canada. However, there remain sensitive questions of political principle as well as questions about potential economic dangers. Unilateral measures to cope with the problems of extra-territoriality would tend to create misunderstanding, ill will, and retaliations. It would seem to be both desirable and feasible for national governments to negotiate agreements with each other about the application of national laws to the various segments of international companies, at least for some of the less emotion-charged areas where national jurisdictions now overlap.

The remaining question is wider than direct investment alone. It is about the consequences for a country's domestic economic policy of greater international mobility of capital. International direct investment and international integration

---

[2]The main public document in the discussion is the Watkins Report. This study was commissioned and published by the Government of Canada; it contains the findings and recommendations of a group of leading Canadian academic economists. Professor Melville Watkins headed the group. The full title of the document is *Foreign Ownership and the Structure of Canadian Industry: Report of the Task Force on the Structure of Canadian Industry* (Ottawa: Prepared for the Privy Council Office, Queen's Printer, 1968).

of capital markets are partly separate topics, but the two processes reinforce each other. What happens to the effectiveness of a nation's fiscal and monetary policies when its capital markets become more closely integrated with the rest of the world? The main point is that these policies do not become unworkable in the face of greater international mobility of capital. Rather, they come to work differently and have to be operated in different ways to reach the same objectives.

AMOUNT OF FOREIGN
DIRECT INVESTMENT IN CANADA

Table 12 shows the degree of Canada's reliance on all kinds of foreign capital for new capital formation. "Use of foreign resources" refers to the net new inflow of foreign funds (equal to the current account deficit) plus savings of foreign-owned firms. "Foreign financing" is gross reliance on foreign funds, not net of outflows of Canadian funds. Although Canadian rates of savings are as high as in similar countries, the very capital-intensive structure of the economy leads to heavy reliance on foreign savings as well.

Table 13 shows the forms which these international investments have taken. About three fifths of foreign long-term investment in Canada is in the form of direct investment.

While foreigners owned $17.2 million of direct investment in Canada at the end of 1965, they controlled $22.9 million of assets. The United States overwhelmingly has provided the largest part of these direct investments—81 per cent of the ownership and 76 per cent of the control. The United Kingdom owns 12 per cent, and almost all of the remaining 7 per cent is owned in Continental Europe. Japan is a special case deserving mention. While Japanese direct investments in Canada are still relatively tiny, they have grown rapidly in recent years. Much more important so far has been what could be considered an alternative to direct investment, namely long-term contracts with Japanese industry for large supplies of Canadian minerals.[3]

Table 14 shows the industrial composition of foreign direct investment in Canada. It is apparent that much of the investment is closely related to natural resources—minerals, oil, and forests. But purely extractive activities represent a minority of the investments; most of them are in processing or manufacturing, and significant amounts are in finance and merchandising.

Table 15 summarizes, for those industries in which foreign direct investment is greatest, the portions of each industry controlled by Canadians and by

---

[3]These contracts are an "alternative to direct investment" in that the Japanese have not taken an equity interest in the local operations.

TABLE 12

Foreign Capital in Canadian Capital Formation

	1954-57	1962-65
	(in per cent)	
Use of Foreign Resrouces as Percentage of:		
Gross Capital Formation	26	20
Net Capital Formation	32	19
Foreign Financing of:		
Gross Capital Formation	31	33
Net Capital Formation	43	43

Source: Canada, Dominion Bureau of Statistics, *The Canadian Balance of International Payments 1963, 1964 and 1965 and International Investment Position.*

TABLE 13

Canadian Balance of International Indebtedness at Year Ends
(millions of dollars)

	1955	1965
Foreign Long-Term Investment in Canada		
Direct Investment	7.7	17.2
Portfolio and Miscellaneous	5.8	12.3
Total	13.5	29.5
Canadian Long-Term Investment Abroad		
Direct Investment	1.7	3.5
Portfolio and Miscellaneous	2.7	4.3
Total	4.4	7.8
Equity of Nonresidents in Canadian		
Assets Abroad	0.7	1.6
Net Short-Term Balance (including		
official reserves)	+1.8	+1.2
Net International Indebtedness (net		
total of all above items)	8.0	22.1
Gross National Product (Year)	27.1	52.1

Source: Canada, Dominion Bureau of Statistics, *The Canadian Balance of International Payments 1963, 1964 and 1965 and International Investment Position.*

TABLE 14

**Foreign Direct Investment in Canada
by Type of Business, End of 1965
(book value in millions of Canadian dollars)**

	All Countries	United States	United Kingdom	All Other Countries
Manufacturing				
Vegetable Products	794	627	147	20
Animal Products	185	171	8	6
Textiles	141	97	42	2
Wood and Paper Products	1,359	1,164	184	11
Iron and Products	3,013	1,769	185	59
Nonferrous Metals	1,112	1,021	58	33
Nonmetallic Minerals	262	160	25	77
Chemicals and Allied Products	1,171	947	182	42
Miscellaneous Manufactures	148	142	5	1
Sub-Total (excluding petroleum refining)	7,185	6,098	836	251
Petroleum and Natural Gas	4,530	3,600	470	460
Other Mining and Smelting	2,018	1,875	100	43
Utilities (excluding pipelines)	306	286	13	7
Merchandising	1,057	695	275	87
Financial	1,685	1,041	261	383
Other Enterprises	427	345	58	24
Total	17,208	13,940	2,013	1,255

Source: Canada, Dominion Bureau of Statistics, *The Canadian Balance of International Payments 1963, 1964 and 1965 and International Investment Position.*

TABLE 15

Nationality of Control of Selected Canadian Industries
(percentages)

	End of 1959			End of 1963		
	Canada	U.S.	Other	Canada	U.S.	Other
Manufacturing	43	44	13	40	46	14
Petroleum and Natural Gas	27	67	6	26	62	12
Other Mining and Smelting	39	53	8	41	52	7
Railways	98	2	0	98	2	0
Other Utilities	95	4	1	96	4	0
Merchandising and Construction	91	6	3	88	7	5
Total	68	26	6	66	27	7

Source: Canada, Dominion Bureau of Statistics, *The Canadian Balance of International Payments 1963, 1964 and 1965 and International Investment Position.*

foreigners. Foreign control is heaviest in manufacturing and in other mining and smelting (where in both cases it covers about three fifths of the assets involved) and in petroleum and natural gas (where it covers three quarters).

PERFORMANCE OF FOREIGN-CONTROLLED FIRMS[4]

There are two a priori reasons for suspecting that foreign-controlled firms might contribute less than they should to the Canadian economy. First of all, there is the possibility that decisions made in the foreign head office may be biased by poor information about Canada or by indifference toward the Canadian portion of the international firm's operations. This reason is based on doubts about the competence of the international firm to manage all of its operations in the most effective way. The other possibility is that even well-made decisions at the head office may conflict with Canadian interests because the global profit of the company may at times require sacrifices by the Canadian subsidiary. This reason reflects an essentially protectionist view, that is, a view that the Canadian subsidiary should be developed even when it is not the most profitable place for the development in question to occur. To illustrate these two points, suppose that a particular subsidiary in Canada is prohibited by its parent from exporting to certain overseas markets because those markets are reserved for other parts of the international firm's production. If the Canadian subsidiary could supply those markets at lower cost than the other plants do, then we can complain about the competence of the head-office management to maximize its global profit; the restriction on the exports of the Canadian subsidiary comes from an error of information or judgment. Alternatively, if the Canadian subsidiary is a higher-cost producer anyhow, we cannot complain that the head-office decision to exclude it from export markets is uneconomic. Our objections would be those of a Canadian protectionist who sees a need for the development of Canadian production even when outside producers are more efficient.

"Performance" of firms refers to a wide variety of actions by which the firms may affect the Canadian economy and even Canadian society in general. The aspects of performance discussed below are: (1) Canadian participation in

---

[4]Much the most thorough investigations of the behavior of foreign-owned firms in Canada have been those by A. E. Safarian. See his *Foreign Ownership of Canadian Industry* (Toronto: McGraw-Hill, 1966). The entire discussion of performance in this chapter is essentially a summary of parts of another study by Safarian, *The Performance of Foreign-Owned Firms in Canada* (Washington, D.C., and Montreal: Canadian-American Committee, forthcoming).

senior positions in subsidiaries, (2) autonomy of subsidiaries in their decision making, (3) external trade of subsidiaries, (4) research and development, (5) financial policies of subsidiaries, and (6) the efficiency of foreign-owned firms.

Canadian Participation in
Senior Positions in Subsidiaries

Canada's best interests in this area are not clear. On the one hand, it is desirable that Canadian citizens be given full opportunity to develop and apply managerial skills, and they should be free to do so within foreign-owned as well as in domestically owned firms. Also, the presence of at least a few Canadians in the management of a subsidiary might make it more responsive to other Canadian objectives for the performance of the firm. On the other hand, the United States has a very large stock of high-quality managers and entrepreneurs. Canada can benefit by drawing upon this U.S. supply of abilities to supplement its own scarce stock. Therefore, "desirable" performance by subsidiaries with respect to Canadian participation in their management would probably avoid either the extreme of complete dominance of subsidiary management by foreigners or the extreme of complete dominance by Canadians.

The available evidence does not tell us what discrimination, if any, there is by nationality in appointments to senior positions in subsidiaries, nor whether the mixture of Canadians and U.S. citizens that has emerged represents an optimum reliance by Canada on foreign supplies of managerial skill. But at least there is a mixture. For example, in 1962 there were 138 corporations in manufacturing, mining, and petroleum, with assets of $25 million or more, and with 50 per cent of their stock owned abroad. In 75 per cent of these companies, the president lived in Canada, and in 45 per cent he was a Canadian citizen. Of the other officers resident in Canada, 706 out of 865 were Canadian citizens. By contrast, in the 79 corporations in these same industries whose stock was mainly held in Canada and which had assets of over $25 million, 91 per cent of the presidents who lived in Canada were Canadian citizens, and 95 per cent of the other officers resident in Canada were Canadian citizens. Canadian participation tends to be greater in the management of those foreign-controlled firms which have a minority of Canadian-held shares, and it tends to be greater in larger firms and in older ones.

Autonomy of Subsidiaries
in Their Decision-Making

Both for the sake of fostering local managerial skills and for the sake of encouraging sensitivity by the firm to special Canadian objectives, the Canadian interest is presumably that the subsidiary firm in Canada should have the greatest possible autonomy. One qualification to this statement is needed—it would of course be harmful to employment and production in Canada if a subsidiary were allowed to fail under the guidance of incompetent but autonomous local management when it could be made to flourish under centralized control from the foreign head office.

In his 1959 survey, Safarian found a wide range of degrees of autonomy in foreign-owned firms, but over half of the firms had "a substantial degree of decentralization."[5] This meant substantial or complete autonomy in such matters as production planning, marketing, and labor relations; major changes in policy and major financial decisions required at least consultation with and approval by the parent. A younger subsidiary tended to be supervised more closely, as was a subsidiary that was an "only child," or one that was in difficulty, or one that produced relatively few products or was involved in substantial vertical integration.

While modern management procedures and communications tend to favor centralization of decision making, there are also pressures for decentralization, especially across national boundaries. There is the need to give local managers a sufficient degree of autonomy to attract competent ones, and there is the need to adapt local decisions to any peculiar features of the local environment. Possibly the strongest pressures toward decentralization in the Canadian case result from Canadian and U.S. tariffs. The tariffs partially segregate the two national markets, discourage vertical integration across the border, and discourage specialization between parents and subsidiaries in their production. Therefore, the tariffs increase the opportunity and even the need for autonomous decision making in the Canadian subsidiaries which are confined mainly to the Canadian market.[6]

External Trade of Subsidiaries

It is sometimes suggested that subsidiary companies in Canada are likely to export too little and import too much. On the exports side, the suggestion is that market-sharing arrangements within an international company may exclude the Canadian subsidiary from certain export markets and especially from the market in which the parent company resides. In the long run, of course, a competently managed profit-maximizing firm would allocate its production to

---

[5] Safarian, *Foreign Ownership of Canadian Industry, op. cit.*

[6] The above is an argument in favor of the tariff. We hasten to add that there are arguments against tariffs, too, but this chapter is not about trade policy.

its most efficient plants, so that there is no reason for foreign ownership to interfere with the location of production according to principles of comparative advantage. In the short run, the parent might restrict sales from particular, efficient subsidiaries in order to protect other existing facilities that have not been fully depreciated. Also, agreements among independent firms to share markets may have adverse effects on particular subsidiaries while benefiting the global profits of the international companies involved.

The Canadian experience is that, in total, foreign-owned companies perform very well as exporters. Of course, we might expect them to do so. They include subsidiaries of the largest multinational corporations, and the orientation of much direct investment in Canada is toward extraction and processing of raw materials for export markets. The propensity to export varies greatly among industries. In 1965, U.S. subsidiaries in Canada in paper and allied products exported 60 per cent of their total sales, whereas in electrical machinery the proportion was 7.5 per cent, and in rubber products, 1.9 per cent. The average for all manufactured goods was 19 per cent. When larger foreign-owned and independent firms producing broadly similar products are compared, there appears to be no difference in the proportion of output exported.

Safarian's 1959 survey, which covered 238 firms on this point, revealed that 39 subsidiaries felt that foreign affiliation aided their exports through better contacts with foreign customers, through guaranteed purchases by affiliates, or through the use of the parent's name, or research, or sales organization. Another 20 firms felt that affiliation retarded their exports because of restrictions on sales to particular countries or because of the existence of affiliates abroad (in some cases including affiliates with lower costs). The rest of the firms—179 of them—said their exports were not affected, for various reasons, such as prohibitive transportation costs or the fact that the company was newly established. (Safarian's survey suggested that licensing arrangements between unrelated parties appeared to be more restrictive of trade than such arrangements between related parties.)[7]

In view of suggestions which we have heard that European firms tend to place direct investments in Canada to produce for export to the United States, we should record that there is little evidence to be found in Canada of such a tendency. U.S. tariffs and distance generally prevent it. Some European firms appear to have used direct investment in Canada as a relatively inexpensive way of testing the North American market, before deciding whether to proceed with investments in the United States. One particular firm is considering a Canadian location from which to export to the United States, because of a combination of low U.S. tariffs and regional-development incentives in Canada.

---

[7] *Ibid.*

Turning to imports, we must remember that foreign direct investments, especially in manufacturing, are often a replacement for exports to the country in which the investment is placed. The question of import performance of subsidiaries, then, is not merely a question of how much the subsidiaries actually import compared with domestically owned firms but also a question of what the nation's imports would have been had the investment not occurred. We might expect subsidiaries to import more than domestically owned firms do, when they are establishing new industry in Canada and have to rely on the parent company for various components and product lines. There would be grounds for complaint if the subsidiaries gave preference to imports over competitive Canadian components and supplies. The parent company might, in the short run, protect an inefficient plant elsewhere by requiring the Canadian subsidiary to import from it; but in the longer run, as inefficient plants wear out, it is in the interests of the global profit of the parent to let all its subsidiaries turn to the lowest-cost suppliers. (It should be noted that this situation can work both ways. In particular cases, it may be the Canadian subsidiary that is the inefficient one receiving short-run protection of its sales to foreign affiliates.)

Safarian's 1959 survey showed that resident-owned firms in general made a larger portion of their purchases in Canada than did nonresident-owned firms. For example, only 31 per cent of resident-owned firms imported over 20 per cent of their purchases of goods and services amenable to international trade, but 53 per cent of nonresident-owned firms did so. Of the sample, 6 per cent (11 firms) reported arrangements such as required purchases of parts from affiliates. Over half of the firms reported no direct effects of affiliation on their imports, and 21 per cent of them reported direct effects that were described as helpful, e.g., imports of standardized parts for a product similar to that of the parent, or contacts with suppliers.[8]

Research and Development

With technological progress receiving increased attention in recent years as an important source of economic growth, a new and sometimes indiscriminate enthusiasm has developed for research and development (R & D). There is some concern in Canada because this country's expenditure on R & D as a percentage of gross national product is only half of that of the United Kingdom and one third that of the United States, and because private business in Canada spends especially little on R & D compared with private business in other advanced countries.

---

[8] *Ibid.*

To appraise the performance of foreign-owned companies with respect to R & D in Canada, it is first necessary to decide what the Canadian interest is in this area, and that itself is a question currently under debate. R & D is not an end in itself; it is only a means toward economic growth,[9] and we can justify any expenditure on it only if the same expenditure would not be more productive in some other direction such as purchase of patent rights, highway construction, retraining of labor, and so on. There are many sources of economic growth, and they compete with each other for the funds available for investment in growth. The pattern of opportunities for growth is surely different from country to country; therefore, the amount spent on R & D in other countries is meaningless as a criterion for what Canada should spend. One important reason why Canada spends relatively little on R & D is that the country has rather full and prompt access to foreign advances in technology through the medium of subsidiaries of foreign companies.

Safarian's 1959 survey indicated that 187 firms of the 215 who reported on the point had full access to the R & D and know how of the parent. Also, 80 per cent of the companies had access to the parent's patents or copyrights, often for no charge or for a nominal payment (although, of course, payment may have been made indirectly).[10] Associated with their access to parent-company research is the fact that Canadian sursidiaries do relatively less research themselves, and especially less basic research, than do their parents. At the same time, foreign-owned companies do a large portion of the research that is done by business in Canada. They tend to be in those industries that are highly research oriented. And they spend at least as much on research per dollar of sales as do similar resident-owned firms, once allowances for type of industry are made.

If we accept the view that Canada's interest is to achieve her technological progress through the most economical mixture of domestic R & D and imported technology, there appears to be no reason to complain about the performance of foreign-owned firms in this area. (This is not to suggest that Canada needs to be or should be completely reliant on foreign R & D. In the production of technology, as in the production of commodities, there are comparative advantages and scope for specialization and exchange.)

Financial Policies of Subsidiaries

Presumably the international company would seek to price its international transactions in order to shift profits into those countries with lower rates of

---

[9] Of course R & D expenditures are also for military strength or national prestige. The above argument, suitably adapted, is relevant to those purposes too.

[10] Safarian, *Foreign Ownership of Canadian Industry, op. cit.*

corporate income tax, while tax authorities in the countries with higher rates would seek to prevent such shifting. There are three respects in which juggling of prices may provide undue cost (or gain) to the Canadian economy. The juggling may involve dumping; it may alter the tax revenue accuring to Canada; and it may affect the earnings of minority Canadian shareholders. There has not been any general study of the pricing of goods and services traded between Canadian subsidiaries and their foreign affiliates, nor has there been any general concern apparent in Canada about these questions.

The great majority of parent companies own all or nearly all of the voting stock of their subsidiaries. They strongly prefer this arrangement, mainly to avoid the complications that the existence of minority shareholdings creates in decisions about financing, location, retention of earnings, and so on. One of the recommendations of the Watkins Report is that stronger incentives be provided for large companies to offer shares to Canadians. The purposes would be to cope with the shortage of equities in Canada, to facilitate disclosure of corporate financial data, and to counter extraterritoriality. However, the report recognized that it would take $4 billion to $5 billion to buy a substantial minority interest in every subsidiary, and argued that most of such an amount would be more useful if put into Canadian-owned enterprise, if necessary through the medium of a government-sponsored "Canada Development Corporation."

As for profits earned by foreign-owned firms, Canada's interest is that these should be no more than sufficient to hold the investments in Canada as efficient operations. The evidence is that foreign-owned firms in general earn a rate of profit about equal to or slightly higher than that of resident-owned firms.

The dividends policy of foreign-owned firms tends to depend on whether there is a minority shareholding. If there is one, the firm usually must establish a regular policy toward distribution of earnings. If the firm is wholly owned by the parent, it is likely to be flexible and erratic in its dividends payments, retaining large or small amounts of its earnings as investment opportunities for them require. In this respect, the closely owned firm is at an advantage over the firm with minority shareholders. The earnings of foreign-owned firms of course are a burden on the Canadian balance of payments when they are distributed, and they represent an automatic growth of foreign ownership when they are not distributed.

The Efficiency of Foreign-Owned Firms

Definite evidence is not available, but it appears that foreign-owned firms are as efficient as resident-owned firms, and in some respects more efficient. At the same time, they are generally less efficient than their foreign parents. Some have lower costs than the parent, usually because of lower wages. Some have about equal costs. But most have higher costs, often because of a smaller scale of production.

Small scale is not a typical problem for firms in the export-oriented resource industries. However, in secondary manufacturing, which is still aimed primarily at the domestic market in Canada, most subsidiaries produce at least a majority of the goods in the parent's product range; therefore, given the size and structure of the Canadian market, they experience short production runs and frequent interruptions while equipment is adjusted to another style or model.

This problem is not an attribute of foreign ownership; it exists for Canadian-owned firms too. The problem is the product of foreign tariffs (which confine Canadian producers to the local market and thus prevent long production runs in particular product lines for export) and Canadian tariffs (which allow this inefficient structure of industry to survive).[11]

While the most important reason for many foreign direct investments in Canada was to get behind the Canadian tariff, there is an increasing opinion in the country that these infant industries have now "grown up" and could face world competition if they could achieve the long production runs that export markets would permit.[12]

EXTRATERRITORIALITY[13]

All the previous discussion of the performance of foreign-owned firms has been on the assumption that the parent company's management has been

---

[11]It is conceivable that even in the absence of tariffs, firms could, through collusion, maintain the same inefficient structure of industry; and participation by foreign-owned subsidiaries in such collusion would tend to protect such arrangements from competition of imports. Thus anticombines policy is also relevant to the problem.

[12]See, for example, H. Edward English, *Industrial Structure in Canada's International Competitive Position* (Montreal: Canadian Trade Committee of the Private Planning Associate of Canada, 1964); and R. J. and Paul Wonnacott, *Free Trade Between the United States and Canada: The Potential Economic Effects* (Cambridge: Harvard University Press, 1967).

[13]This section is based primarily on the Watkins Report, whose recommendations involve a firm rejection of extraterritoriality. The present discussion is also indebted to a forthcoming commentary by H. Edward English and to Harry Johnson, "Towards a New National Policy?" *International Journal*, (Autumn, 1968). An excellent concise study of the topic is Kingman Brewster, Jr., *Law and United States Business in Canada* (Washington, D.C. and Montreal: Canadian-American Committee, 1960).

UNIVERSITY OF VICTORIA
LIBRARY
Victoria, B. C.

pursuing the best interests of the whole company as a private, profit-seeking concern. A net set of issues arises when we turn to the application of the laws, guidelines, or directives of foreign governments, through the parent companies, to their subsidiaries resident in Canada.

While the economic effects of foreign ownership are amenable to a cool-headed calculation of costs and benefits, infringements of national sovereignty through the extraterritorial application of foreign law are not. Therefore, we begin this discuussion by seeking to separate the emotional symbols from the practical substance of the issue.

Absolute legal sovereignty, defined as the exclusive right to make all the laws that apply in its territory, is a symbol of a nation's nationhood. Sovereignty is different from independence, which is the freedom to choose and carry out preferred policies. Independence is never complete, especially not in today's interdependent world. To emphasize the difference between symbolic sovereignty and effective independence, we might point out that it is conceivable for a nation to preserve a symbolic sovereignty, by making all its own laws, while losing some actual independence, because some of those laws are made in response to foreign pressures. Also, a nation may lose some sovereignty by accepting extraterritorial application of some foreign laws but retain independence if the acceptance is voluntary and reversible. At the same time, insistence on symbolic sovereignty can be an important weapon in a struggle to maximize effective independence, especially for a weaker nation facing a stronger one. The following discussion of extraterritoriality is based on the premise that Canada's interest is not to insist on absolute, symbolic sovereignty for its own sake but rather to strive for the greatest possible degree of effective independence to pursue real national goals. From this point of view, extraterritoriality can be discussed in terms of a balance between benefits and costs.

While the question of extraterritoriality arises in principle with all foreign direct investments, all the discussion of it in Canada and in this chapter relates to direct investments that come from the United States.

The particular case of extraterritoriality that has caused the greatest public concern in Canada is the U.S. prohibition against trade by U.S. companies and their subsidiaries with China, North Korea, North Vietnam, and (with qualifications) Cuba. The regulations apply to any company with 50 per cent or more of its shares owned in the United States. U.S. directors and shareholders are liable to prosecution in the United States for violations by their subsidiaries. The phrase "automobiles for Red China" has become a somewhat emotive one in Canada as a result of one well-publicized incident, although the U.S. subsidiary involved has denied that there ever was a Chinese order for automobiles. Canadian emotions seem to have congealed around the wrong commodity; it is unlikely that China is a potentially important market for North American cars, but it may be a promising market for potash and flour. It is not possible to measure the amount of potential Canadian exports that have in fact been foregone because of the restraints on U.S.-owned subsidiaries, but there are reasons to suppose that the economic costs to Canada may have been fairly unimportant. The political aspects of the situation are more disturbing. Of course political stances have to be subjected to cost-benefit analysis as well as to economic policies, and there are trade-offs for Canada between different policy objectives, for instance, between friendly relations with the United States and exclusive jurisdiction over foreign-owned firms. But perhaps this is an area in which Canada needs to emphasize its absolute sovereignty in order to prevent erosion of its relative independence.

Various efforts have been made to work out compromises. The Eisenhower-Diefenbaker Joint Statement on Export Policies, in 1958, recognized the general problem and agreed to full consultation to find "solutions to concrete problems as they arise." U.S. authorities have made specific concessions in the form of case-by-case exemptions when it can be shown that there is a firm order from a Communist country for goods that cannot be supplied by a Canadian-owned firm and that the order is of importance to the Canadian economy.[14] While this procedure may look after the largest part of the economic problems involved for Canada, at the political level it is an unpalatable compromise for both countries. The United States finds itself exempting particular U.S. citizens from U.S. law at Canada's request, while Canada finds itself asking the United States for permission to fill certain export orders. Such a compromise could hardly be workable save against a background of exceptional good will on both sides.

In 1965, the Merchant-Heeney Report, "Canada and the United States, Principles for Partnership," was released. It had been prepared in relation to a meeting between President Lyndon B. Johnson and Prime Minister Lester B. Pearson. It recommended what would be the ideal solution for Canada to the problem of extraterritorial extension of U.S. export controls, namely, that U.S. subsidiaries in Canada be fully exempted from the controls. This recommendation has fallen into neglect.

The Watkins Report suggested what it described as a second-best solution, assuming the ideal solution for Canada is not attainable. It proposed a government agency empowered to receive export orders from certain foreign countries and to require private producers to sell to it the goods with which to fill the orders. The economic gains that would emerge would depend on the volume of trade that resulted, and this might well be small. The value of the agency would perhaps be primarily as a symbolic assertion of sovereignty. The

---

[14]These concessions are the main basis for the supposition in the previous paragraph that "the economic costs to Canada may have been fairly unimportant." For example, given the possibility of a concession, one can suppose that, if the Chinese wanted much potash, a large and firm order would be forthcoming, and that U.S.-owned firms would be allowed to fill it. But of course all this is suppositious—some commentators would say supposititious.

cost of such an assertion would be the annoyance of those in the United States who would see it as a challenge to U.S. sovereignty over U.S. companies and as a show of disloyalty to the Western Alliance. The potential for misunderstanding and ill will that unilateral solutions to this problem create emphasizes the need for cooperative efforts to solve it.

Economically the most important impact on Canada of extraterritoriality has been the effects of the U.S. balance-of-payments programs. In 1965, the United States introduced its program of voluntary restraints for U.S. businesses to encourage them to adjust their international operations in order to improve the U.S. balance of payments, and at the end of that year revised the program to include a specific guideline to limit direct investment. The Canadian response included certain measures to discourage new borrowing in Canada by U.S. firms, and official discussions which led in March, 1966, to what was apparently an informal exemption of Canada from the program. Canada also issued a set of guiding principles to subsidiary companies as a device of moral suasion and began collecting statistics on the operations of these firms. After the United States introduced its stiffer and mandatory program at the beginning of 1968, the Canadian dollar came under strong pressure; the crisis was ended only by agreement that the United States would entirely exempt Canada from the program. In exchange, Canada took measures to avoid becoming a so-called pass through for U.S. funds to other countries.

Several points can be made about this experience. One is that Canada's heavy reliance on U.S. direct investments has in a sense worked in Canada's own favor in these episodes. Countries less vulnerable to damage by the guidelines and mandatory restraints have had to accept them. Canada has been able to gain exemption from them, mainly because of her vulnerability, but also, to a degree, because of some reverse flow of influence, from the Canadian subsidiaries, through the U.S. parent companies, to the U.S. Government.

Another point is that the whole problem of the extraterritorial impact of the U.S. balance-of-payments guidelines and restraints exists only because those measures exist. In other words, reliance on domestic monetary and fiscal policies and exchange-rate adjustments to cure persistent balance-of-payments problems would prevent this aspect of extraterritoriality from appearing. This wider question should be included in the discussion of whether rigid exchange rates are more conducive to international investment than are more flexible ones.

A third point is that the Canadian solution to the problems posed by the U.S. balance-of-payments program as it applies to U.S. subsidiaries is not generally applicable to other countries. Canada has been granted almost complete exemption from the U.S. programs and has in return taken measures to prevent the U.S. program's being frustrated by passage of U.S. funds through Canada to other countries. In effect, Canada has joined something approaching the nature of a "common exchange-control area" with the United States. While this involves a far wider set of issues than the question of foreign direct investment and extraterritoriality, it has solved the latter problem for Canada. But what is a preferable solution for Canada is the only solution for the rest of the world—namely, international negotiations and agreement on the division among national governments of jurisdiction over international companies.

The third main area where U.S. law extends into Canada through U.S. subsidiaries is antitrust. U.S. law, or at least its enforcement, is more severe than is Canadian. In some cases, for example, when there are U.S. prohibitions against participation by U.S. subsidiaries in Canadian patent pools, or market-sharing agreements, or price collusion, the effects may be a beneficial increase in competition in Canada. In other cases, especially with respect to corporate mergers that would help to rationalize Canadian production, U.S. prohibition may be harmful to the Canadian economy.[15]

The Watkins Report has suggested several second-best steps that Canada could take to bar U.S. antitrust law from Canada. They are second best in that they are unilateral, while the ideal solution would be international agreements. One step would be prohibition against removal of business records from Canada by reason of a foreign court order. Another would be collection of more information about the actual incidence and effect in Canada of U.S. antitrust law. A third would be legislation actually prohibiting compliance in Canada with foreign antitrust orders, decrees, and judgments.

Some Canadians criticize the strong stand taken by the Watkins Report on extraterritoriality. One of their criticisms is that the report has not followed through the implications of the difference between legal sovereignty and actual independence. They suggest that the report gives exaggerated importance to the outward trappings of legal sovereignty. They would prefer a much more pragmatic approach to the problems of extraterritoriality, including a willingness to accept it where it appears to be good law for Canada (as in certain aspects of antitrust) and a general preference for problem-by-problem negotiation and compromise rather than unilateral action.

The Watkins Report and its critics tend to disagree on what the second-best solutions to extraterritoriality would be. However, there is widespread agreement that the ideal solution would be an international, preferably multilateral, convention about the legal status and responsibility of the international company (preferably, of course, giving full and exclusive jurisdiction to each nation over all its residents). It may be futile to ask for an international code on all aspects of extraterritoriality—for example, questions of "trading with the enemy" may be too delicate to open. But it would be a very useful beginning if even a few of the more technical questions—such as taxation and antitrust law—could be dealt with in this way.

---

[15] See Brewster, *op. cit.*, pp. 7–10, 15ff.

INCREASED INTERNATIONAL MOBILITY
OF CAPITAL

Recent work, both theoritical and empirical, has shed light on the consequences of greater international mobility of capital for the effectiveness of the domestic economic policies of a nation.[16] Mobility of capital is a topic that overlaps in part the topic of foreign direct investment and because of the overlap is briefly discussed here. New international direct investments are themselves a form of capital movement, and new and existing direct investments create and widen channels for the international movement of other forms of capital.

Increased international mobility of capital, i.e., greater integration among national capital markets, reduces a nation's ability to control its own level and structure of interest rates. For example, the attempt to impose a restrictive monetary policy and higher interest rates leads to capital inflows, and the inflows limit the increase in interest rates and partly frustrate the official efforts to restrict the supply of loans. But that is not the end of the story. To the extent that monetary policy is made less effective in its direct impact on domestic activity, it is made more effective in its ability to directly improve the balance of payments and thus in its usefulness as an instrument to defend a fixed exchange rate. If the exchange rate is flexible, the capital inflow will tend to cause appreciation and thus to restrain exports and encourage imports. These current-account effects in turn affect the level of domestic activity. One empirical test has indicated that, given the structure of the Canadian economy, monetary policy has several times more impact on Gross National Product via this sequence than it does via its direct impact on investment spending.

Fiscal policy is also affected by high international mobility of capital. A restrictive fiscal policy (with the money supply held constant to exclude the workings of monetary policy which have already been discussed) means a small government deficit or a larger surplus, and thus, lower interest rates, because the government is borrowing less or repaying more in capital markets. With capital mobile across national boundaries, the fall in domestic interest rates is limited by the fact that funds will flow out of the country to avoid the fall. Thus, the effectiveness of fiscal policy is increased; that is, the restraint caused by fiscal policy would have been partly offset by the resultant lowering of interest rates had capital not been so mobile out of the country. This is a significant effect,

---

[16]See, in particular, R. A. Mundell, "Capital Mobility and Stabilization Policy under Fixed and Flexible Exchange Rates," *Canadian Journal of Economics and Political Science*, (November, 1963); and R. E. Caves and G. L. Reuber, *Canadian Economic Policy and the Impact of International Capital Flows*, PPAC series, Canada in the Atlantic Economy (Toronto: University of Toronto Press, forthcoming). The empirical tests referred to in the text are from the latter.

according to one empirical test, which showed that the effectiveness of fiscal policy would be 5 to 30 per cent greater in Canada with internationally mobile capital than without it, under a fixed exchange rate. Under a flexible exchange rate, the situation is different again. As restrictive fiscal policy leads to lower interest rates and capital outflows, the exchange rate depreciates and the restrictive effects of the fiscal measures are impaired by the resulting stimulus through external trade.

The conclusion to be drawn from the foregoing brief sampling of the topic is that monetary and fiscal policies are not frustrated by the existence of a high degree of international mobility of capital. Rather, their workings are changed, and they can still be used to achieve domestic objectives, provided that their new workings are properly understood.

7 RECOMMENDATIONS AND SUMMARY

RECOMMENDATIONS

On the basis of the background papers and discussion presented at the Conference on Direct Investment in the Atlantic Area (Chapters 1–6), the conference recognized that a new world economy is taking shape largely as the result of a trend toward the internationalization of production.

The volume of goods and services resulting from international investment has bypassed exports, and its present growth rate is considerably larger than that of international trade, thus making international investment the major channel of international economic relations. The international corporation is the main expression of this unprecedented phenomenon. Investment across national boundaries is largely a reflection of the development of technology, and affects every facet of the established order—financial, cultural, and political.

The economic consequences of foreign direct investment are held almost universally to be beneficial. The process expands the total of world investment and production. It is a strong factor for economic integration and brings about a better allocation of resources throughout the developed world.

But as international investment solves old problems, it raises new ones. Significant obstacles of a psychological, political, or economic nature exist, limiting or distorting the international investment procedure.

The Role of International Corporations

The conference discussed what the international corporations and the governments might do in order to reduce a number of these obstacles. Its recommendations on four basic areas are stated below.

First, the international corporations have to take full account of the policies, conditions, and aspirations of each country in which they are established. To do so is an essential of good management. The fears that exist in some countries about these corporations can best be allayed by better disclosure and publicity of corporate activity, including financial data, and by a greater effort in explaining the corporation's long-range goals, policies, and involvement in each nation's life.

Second, it is desirable that the governments of the Atlantic nations and Japan should take action to remove, in the most liberal and effective way, those obstacles which hamper transnational direct investment and develop rules of good behavior for both base and host countries to avoid the use of international corporations as instruments of national political policies by base countries and to avoid discrimination by host countries inconsistent with a reasonable exercise of national sovereignty.

The conference recommended to their respective governments full support of the principle of an international code under international sponsorship, including a reasonable statement of the obligations of investors and of host and base countries.

The focus of interest in the conference was on direct investment. However, the conference was aware that trade policy, customs barriers, the use of artificial incentives, monetary policy, financial integration, double taxation of corporate income, and other related factors were inseparable from the problem of direct investment in formulating government policy. These problems cannot be solved unilaterally, or even bilaterally, but only in a multinational framework.

Third, the conference concluded that the international capital market could no longer be regarded only as a sibstitute market and should be regarded as permanent. The recognition of that fact by governments, monetary authorities, and others would tend to keep the market free from unilateral interference taken without full consideration of the impact of any one nation's action on that market. Appropriate procedures should be developed, as a matter of urgency, to encourage multilateral discussion to assure maximum freedom of international capital flows.

Finally, the international capital market has grown without government surveillance. The conference recommended that the responsible banks and issuing houses exercise necessary care in order to ensure that it can continue to function in this way.

European Investment in the United States

The conference dedicated particular attention to European direct investment in the United States. It felt that such transactions are highly beneficial both to the United States and to Europe in economic terms, and may, in the short run, contribute to the balance-of-payments adjustment process. The overriding motive for investment is the existence of a vast, dynamic, and sophisticated U.S. market. The conference also felt that direct investment in the U.S. by European companies would tend to balance the reactions against U.S. investment in Europe. Obstacles to investment in this market do exist, and to reduce them the following recommendations to the U.S. Government were made:

First, visa regulations should be eased to avoid the difficulties which currently arise in the employment and utilization of noncitizen management and technical personnel. Modification of the Selective Service System to exempt foreign personnel at work temporarily (up to five years) in the United States was urged.

Second, legal insecurity which stems from the action of U.S. antitrust enforcement authorities should be diminished. The conference concluded that great restraint should be used in extraterritorial application of the antitrust laws. The business review procedures of the antitrust enforcement authorities should be improved. Decisions should be rendered promptly and should be binding over a reasonable length of time. It is recommended that a clear statement of antitrust policy and the principles guiding its application be made available by the competent authorities.

Third, tax regulations should be amended to eliminate discriminatory taxation on those coparticipations in which U.S. companies own less than 80 per cent. The current law permits the filing of a consolidated return only when U.S. participation is 80 per cent or more. This inhibits a more equal distribution of the capital between the U.S. and foreign investors and thus tends to inhibit investment.

Fourth, the conference recognized and approved the stated intention of the present Administration to reduce and eventually remove the Interest Equalization Tax, as soon as conditions permit. In the meantime, consideration should be given to freeing from that tax issues and/or borrowings in the United States by non-U.S. corporations, if the proceeds are used in the United States for direct-investment purposes. Transactions of this kind should be clearly identifiable as such.

Fifth, after taking into consideration the usefulness of the presence of foreign banks in the United States to enhance the environment for direct investment from abroad, the conference recommended that U.S. banking laws be reviewed in order to encourage and facilitate the establishment and operation of foreign bank branches or subsidiaries. In this respect, it is also recommended that the One Bank Holding Act, if enacted, take cognizance of the special position of foreign banks having subsidiaries in the United States.

Two recommendations were directed to European governments: First, all efforts to bring about stronger economic, financial, and market integration in

Europe should be actively encouraged. The European nations should take such steps as are necessary to eliminate the barriers to transnational mergers, to allow European companies to reach dimensions to become more effective competitors in the expanded world markets, and to make international direct investments. Second, certain tax reforms are desirable: Among others, foreign direct-investment income should not be penalized by the use of discriminatory tax legislation in the country of the parent.

SUMMARY

Broadly speaking two major themes comprised the conference discussion. First, that phenomenon which has been called the internationalization of production, and its instrument, the international corporation, was discussed in general, and more specifically the Canadian and Western European responses. This discussion flowed especially from Chapters 1, 5, and 6, which were originally written for the conference and second, the prospects of greater direct investment from Europe and other investors into the United States, the discussion of which flowed from Chapters 2 and 3.

The recommendations of the conference were framed under these two major headings and so, too, is this conference summary.

First, the conference concurred with the major burden of the argument in Chapter 1. That argument may be summarized as follows: Owing to the extension of production beyond national borders, a process begun at the turn of the century, and, after an interwar interruption, now in full flower, a new world economy is taking shape. In magnitude, the volume of goods and services produced as a result of international direct investment has bypassed exports as the major channel of international economic relations. Moreover its growth rate in the past, and probably in the future, outstrips by a considerable margin that of international trade. In aggregate terms, by an OECD estimate, the total volume of international direct investment in 1966 was about $90 billion; $55 billion of this originated in the United States and $35 billion in all of the other countries of Western Europe, Canada, and Japan.

The international corporation is the main expression of this phenomenon. It is through the international corporation that direct investment is carried on. International corporations are difficult to tabulate because of the paucity of statistics, particularly among smaller companies. But it would seem that about 75–85 U.S. companies and a similar number of non-U.S. companies large enough to be listed among the *Fortune* "200 Largest" qualify. There are many definitions of an international company; a widely accepted one is a company which has a 25 per cent or greater foreign content, defined as assets, employment, or income engendered from production abroad.

The defensive motive of the international corporations in going abroad is to get behind tariff barriers, but a more positive motive is to capture and hold a share of a foreign market, a task best accomplished by local production and one apt to continue where tariff barriers to be reduced below their present levels. It is the expansion of technology—including such factors as the ease of communication and travel, the expanded managerial capability of the corporation, and the spreading of new techniques to all markets of the developed world—which is at the root of the movement. Therefore, it is a movement apt to increase with time, and in doing so, to affect every facet of the established order—financial, cultural, and political.

The economic consequences of foreign direct investment are held almost universally to be beneficial. The process expands the total of world investment and production. The major consequence of this expansion is economic integration, that is, a tendency to equalize wage and interest rates, the level of technological development of an economy, and standards of living throughout the developed world. This international integration is an extension on the international scene of the integration process of national economies which took place in earlier decades. In the course of extending beyond their borders, the international corporations bring about a better allocation of resources in the developed world.

But while these benefits are generally recognized, there are certain negative values attached to the process which cannot be ignored. The extension of the international corporation creates an international dimension of economic behavior that threatens the degree to which any individual nation state can control its economic destiny. In large measure, the internationalization of production threatens the sense of political sovereignty and psychological security of the individual nation state. But the threat goes deeper: Local producers resist the international corporations whom they fear as more effective competitors in product, financial, and labor markets. In consequence, local producers induce their governments to establish restrictions against them. The governments as well fear that their control over monetary policy, over local social security or employment policies, perhaps over local plans and exports policies may also be threatened by the introduction of foreign-owned economic units responding in the last analysis to direction from a center outside the host nation. The conferees also noted that the fear of foreign investment even extends to "the mass opinion." And this is ironic, because, in the last analysis, it is the workers of any nation who are most benefited from the increase of foreign investment: It is to these people that the benefits of higher wages accrue, reflecting the greater use of capital to labor, and, hence, higher productivity in the more advanced industries. Indeed, the conferees were told that the resistance to foreign investment resides less in the knowledgeable sectors of society than in the relatively less-informed sectors, who stand to benefit most from the procedure.

In the case of Canada and Western Europe, however, these fears have been mitigated by the observations of current practice. Very few of the practices feared have been observable in fact. Testimony from Canada indicated that the international corporations, largely originating in the United States, have behaved as excellent corporate citizens. The fears that international investment creates for Canadian sovereignty, expressed in the Watkins Report, were dismissed as "illogical." It was pointed out that none of the suggestions of the Watkins Report has been seriously considered as legislation, and, in general, that report was held to reflect the political biases of its authors rather than the real concerns of the Canadian business or consuming classes.

In the case of Western Europe as well, much the same response has held in recent years. The conferees concurred with Dr. Hellman's conclusion in Chapter 5 that the major benefits of international investment to Europe are the rapid extension of technological capabilities, even in the period when much of the capital for U.S. investment in Europe has been raised within Europe itself. However, some conferees found the distinction between "new investment" as opposed to "takeovers" somewhat irrational. If the international corporation improves the allocation of resources and brings the other benefits noted, does it really matter whether the process takes place via takeovers or otherwise? Indeed, there can be no takeover without a willing seller.

Nevertheless, the conference concluded that these fears continue and create obstacles to the international investment procedure. Moreover, other fears were expressed with respect to the future. The conference questioned three points expressed in Chapter 1 in this respect. First, many felt that future international production would be carried out by a relatively small number of companies—300 or 400 is the usual figure put forward. The fact that existing technological leads give way in time to standardized production, encouraging smaller units to compete, was admitted to be true. But, on the other hand, the larger units, through their research capabilities, produce "an envelope of technology" developing new leads as the old ones become standardized. This gives the larger companies an attacking edge and makes for greater concentration. Whether or not European companies will develop to the size necessary for them to compete on this international dimension was held to depend on the speed with which transnational mergers take place in Europe. This in turn depends on the speed with which the nations of the EEC develop either a European company law or some tolerable facsimile such as the elimination of double taxation in the event of merger to permit transnational mergers. Second, the idea was questioned that the aforementioned distribution of international investment, $55 billion from the United States versus $35 billion other, constitutes a balance in the world as it reflects the relative economic capabilities of the regions involved. In any real sense, Western Europe is not a region. Each nation still sees itself as an individual David facing Goliath in the form of the United States. But the speed with which European integration goes forward was also noted so that Western Europe becomes more of an entity, capable of taking advantage of its expanded markets, and this depends entirely on the European will itself. Third, the idea that portfolio and direct-investment totals can be considered jointly in assessing the relative positions of the United States and Western Europe was rejected. Each region has some $22 billion of assets invested in the other. But the bulk of U.S. investment is direct in plant and equipment, and the two were held not to be really comparable.

Pursuant to discussion along these lines, the first two recommendations were made. In essence, these recommendations state a strong preference for the continuation of direct international investment and look to devices to remove obstacles which reduce or distort the process. Pursuant to this thinking, the first recommendation specifically denied that a "code of good behavior" was necessary for international corporations. But it did urge the international corporations to publicize their affairs, and particularly their financial data, and to undertake an educational program to remove the air of mystery which sometimes surrounds them. In this context, it may be significant that some of the European spokesmen pointed to the benefits which had accrued to them from revelation of their financial statistics. In two cases, companies had been forced to reveal these data pursuant to Securities and Exchange Commission regulations in the United States, when they floated shares on the New York Stock Exchange. But the consequence of this move, although the companies undertook it reluctantly at the outset, was to dispel fears at home about their operations as facts were substituted for speculation. In one case, these facts were also used as a basis for negotiations with local unions which tended on the whole to believe U.S. inspired statistics whereas they had been more dubious of previous company assertions.

The rejection of the idea of a code of good behavior for corporations takes into account the fact that such a code is apt in fact to establish maximum rather than minimim standards. Some corporations, elephantine in size, were said to behave with the "grace of a ballerina"; smaller ones, however, were sometimes more abrasive in their behavior. It is really part of the task of good management to behave in conformity with the conditions and aspirations of the host country. It is also part of the task of good management to recruit personnel from all sources on the sole criterion of personal ability rather than race or country of origin.

The second recommendation, however, did propose a "code of good behavior" for governments. The burden of the argument here lay in the fact that governments all too often take unilateral actions which tend to disturb the whole international equilibrium. In other areas, for example, trade policy through the General Agreement on Tariffs and Trade (GATT), there have been multinational agreements that no one nation can in fact disturb the multi-national equilibrium by unilateral action. But there is no similar agreement for the corpus of international agreements to protect capital flows—now a more important channel of economic relations. Earlier attempts to introduce freedom of capital flows, for example the Havana Charter, never materialized. It is now time, the conferees felt, to undertake multinational discussion to assure freedom of capital flows. In this context, it is significant that the conferees distinctly recognized the limited power of any one nation state to control the international dimension, but they were reluctant to indicate through what channel international cooperation should take place. The OECD provides such a tribunal, but the conferees did not wish to restrict multinational movement to any single channel.

Also in this context, the conferees recognized that it is naive to look to the protection of capital movements alone without consideration of other facets of economic policy. In consequence, the proposed multinational approach to the problem should tend to be more global, taking into account considerations of monetary policy, trade policy, the use of customs barriers and artificial incentives to investment, and, in general, that interlocked panoply of policies, all of which feed the international investment process.

The conference rejected the idea that such a multinational framework would be helped by creating a special legal situation for international companies, as this might lead to a position where these companies would appear to be, rightly or wrongly, in a favored position. On the other hand, it is clear that such a framework should be directed toward avoiding discrimination expressly against the same international corporations.

The third recommendation of the conference extended the desire for free capital flows to the international capital market. Originally considered a substitute market, the Euro-bond market, and markets related to it—the Euro-dollar and the sale of securities—must now be regarded as permanent by governmental and monetary authorities of the developed nations. If this principle is recognized, it would be more difficult for any one nation to take unilateral action which tends to distort the operation of the international capital market. In the past, the international capital market developed in large measure to supply the financial needs of U.S. companies operating abroad. But in early 1969, the largest borrowers in it were European companies. While it was admitted that one quarter does not make a trend, it was also contended that the international capital market has now become the place where savers and borrowers meet, and that its future usefulness, in the event of transnational corporate mergers within Europe, would vastly extend to the benefit of European companies. It was further held that even if the New York and London capital markets should reopen fully, the international capital market would continue to hold an important and perhaps predominant place among the world's capital markets. In short, the code of good behavior for governments should be extended to the international capital market.

The banks and other institutions which make this market have in the past done so successfully without governmental surveillance. It is highly desirable that this state of affairs should continue in future, but if this is to be so, the responsible banks and issuing houses should exercise necessary care in order to ensure its free operation.

The special case of Japan was noted in previous chapters. Time did not permit an exhaustive analysis of this unique and interesting case, but the conference agreed that the future lay in a greater integration of the Japanese and other developed economies. This implies that the codes of good government behavior, including the free exchange of capital, should also apply to the Japanese. On their part, Japanese spokesmen restated their intent to free capital movements and restated steps which had been taken to assure that this would be completed by 1972. Discriminations specifically for or against the Japanese economy are now outdated, and governments and the business community should recognize this.

The conference also paid particular attention to European direct investment in the United States. A number of European companies which had been long established in the U.S. market testified to their success and satisfaction with their operations in that country. The economic results evidenced by "our bank account" are self-evident and highly satisfactory. In this context, it was noted that even a small share of the U.S. market is significant; 2 per cent of the U.S. market is equivalent to 50 per cent of the market of a Latin American country. The regional nature of U.S. markets makes it possible for a company to operate at any degree of intensity it wishes, up to and including the whole of the U.S. market. But in addition to these purely economic benefits, several of the European companies cited the technological feedbacks throughout their international operations which they gained from the U.S. experience. In the intensely competitive and advanced U.S. markets, marketing techniques as well as research capabilities were developed which tended to be adapted elsewhere and be fruitful in other areas as well.

But if satisfaction was universally expressed by those who had been established in the U.S. market, what about new potential entrants? The desire of the U.S. authorities, particularly the Department of Commerce, that foreign corporations should make direct investment in the United States was evident is shown in Appendix A of this volume. But the views of the Department of Commerce were assailed as too facile and overlooking a number of genuine obstacles to further European investment in the United States.

The recommendations developed by the conference were designed to remove these obstacles and directed largely to U.S. Government authorities. These recommendations are quite explicit and require further commentary only in several specific instances.

Perhaps the major impediment to European investment in the United States if the fear of U.S. antitrust laws, and this fear takes two forms. The first is the fear that the extraterritorial application of these laws will make European companies vulnerable even in their non-U.S. operations if they also operate in the United States. This fear was expressed very clearly in Chapter 3, and the theoretical possibility of the application of U.S. laws abroad does exist. Yet, in practice, as a number of participants observed, these laws are rarely applied. A cursory comparison of the number of cases of extraterritorial application as well as the already existing number of companies operating in the United States indicates that the theoretical possibility of application is in reality applied only rarely. Nevertheless, the fear continues. By way of reply, Chapter 4 was originally prepared as an appended part of this conference record. This chapter notes that the preservation of a competitive economy makes the entry of European companies possible, and that once these companies undertake U.S. operations, they are treated without discrimination under the same laws that apply to U.S. companies. Moreover, the decisions rendered by the courts, which in fact comprise the essence of U.S. antitrust laws, reflect an increasing awareness that U.S. law must be applied abroad gingerly, if at all, where different circumstances prevail. The increased use of measures to enforce competition in other countries also continues to reduce the disparity between U.S. and foreign law.

The second factor of the antitrust law to which foreign business has objected is the uncertainty of its application. Foreign business, it is alleged, never knows where it stands, even after undertaking operations in the United States. However, in this context, the business review procedures of the antitrust authorities were cited. These procedures are capable of telling foreign investors in advance what they may and may not do, and the effect of a decision is binding even from one Administration to the next. The conferees concurred that these procedures are useful in inducing foreign investment. They suggested that these might be improved, and also suggested that the Department of Justice prepare a booklet outlining specifically how it proceeds in these matters, and that this booklet should be distributed to potential foreign investors. It iis essential that U.S. antitrust procedures be demystified. The author of Chapter 4 agreed to cooperate with other U.S. authorities in the preparation of such a booklet.

As further aids to foreign investment in the United States, other steps should also be undertaken. Immigration and visa regulations are now too strict and stand in the way of the recruitment of foreign managerial and technical personnel. The extension of European banking in the United States would specifically assist the extension of foreign direct investment as well. It is quite natural that foreign businessmen would turn to their own banks for advice and financial assistance. A number of laws, including state banking regulations, now make the extension of foreign banking into the United States difficult. These discriminatory laws should be reduced and eliminated where possible. It may even be necessary to take account of special situations in which some foreign banks find themselves, particularly in the application of the One Bank Holding Law. Similarly, the conference looked to the early elimination of the Interest

Equalization Tax. Even prior to that time, it was thought to be helpful if this tax could be relaxed for the borrowings or share issues of European companies where the proceeds are directly invested in the United States. Is is admittedly difficult to follow the path of the use of monies through the intricate web of financial flows. But it is not impossible that such exemptions from the Interest Equalization Tax could be clearly identifiable to stimulate the foreign-investment procedure. At the same time, it was held desirable that European governments should on their part eliminate barriers to direct investment in the United States. Among other elements which create such barriers, the slowness of European governments in permitting transnational mergers was cited. Some governments apply discriminatory taxes to income earned abroad, and this discourages the international investment procedure and should be eliminated. It was also suggested that governments might take into cognizance the possibility of a consolidated balance-sheet approach to foreign investment. In this case, if losses were incurred at the outset as a result of foreign investment, they should be deductible against earnings elsewhere. Such double-taxation provisions as still have not been eliminated by bilateral treaties should be eliminated. Hopefully hereto a multinational convention might be undertaken to eliminate the unfair and inhibiting incidence of taxation on investment.

APPENDIXES

A

A SUMMARY VIEW OF FOREIGN DIRECT INVESTMENT IN THE UNITED STATES

U.S. Department of Commerce,
Bureau of International Commerce

U.S. Government and business leaders have long recognized the economic, technological, and balance-of-payments benefits that accrue from direct invest-ment in the United States by overseas entrepreneurs. This view, and the official policy it has engendered, date from the beginning of the Republic: In 1791, Alexander Hamilton, the first Secretary of the U.S. Treasury, stated that foreign capital

> Instead of being viewed as a rival . . . ought to be considered as a most valuable auxiliary, conducing to put in motion a greater quantity of productive labor, and a greater portion of useful enterprise, than could exist without it.

The U.S. Government has continued through the years to pursue this open policy toward foreign investment. Its most recent affirmation came in 1961, when the U.S. Department of Commerce established a program designed specifically to encourage a greater flow of direct capital investment to the United States. As part of this program, a special industrial development attaché was assigned to the U.S. Embassy in Paris. His role is to encourage and facilitate investment in the United States by European entrepreneurs. Corresponding activities were initiated in the United States with a view to acquainting the U.S. business community with the prospective opportunities and advantages of association with foreign firms interested in investing in the United States.

INVESTMENT PROFILE

The total value of foreign direct investment in the United States, which amounted to approximately $3.4 billion in 1950, increased to $9.9 billion by 1967 (the most recent year for which data are available). The levels of foreign investment in the United States in recent years and the countries from which investments were made are shown in Table 16. The profile of foreign investment in the United States at the end of 1967, in terms of industry and country of origin, is set forth in Table 17. The year-end data shown in Tables 16 and 17 reflect a number of investment adjustments such as the revaluation of equity securities. The trend of foreign investment in the United States as measured by annual capital inflows and reinvested earnings is shown in Table 18. *New* investment in the United States, defined as the first capital inflow to establish a new company or operations in the United States or to acquire additional shares of existing companies, reveals a similar pattern of expansion between 1965 and 1967 as shown in Table 19. A further substantial increase is indicated for 1968.

TABLE 16

**Foreign Direct Investment in the United States,
Value at Year End
(billions of dollars)**

Country/Region	1950	1965	1966	1967
Canada	1.0	2.4	2.4	2.6
United Kingdom	1.2	2.9	2.9	3.2
Belgium	nss	.2	.2	.2
France	nss	.2	.2	.3
Germany	nss	.2	.2	.3
Italy	nss	.1	.1	.1
Netherlands	.3	1.3	1.4	1.5
Sweden	nss	.2	.2	.2
Switzerland	.3	.9	.9	1.1
Japan	nss	.1	.1	.1
Latin America	nss	.2	.2	.2
Other	nss	.2	.2	.2
Total	3.4	8.8	9.1	9.9

nss = not shown serarately
Details may not add to totals due to rounding.
Source: U.S. Department of Commerece, *Survey of Current Business* (September, 1967; October, 1968).

Finally, a summary of the factors affecting the position of foreign investors in the United States in 1965, 1966, and 1967 is presented in Table 20.

TABLE 17

Value of Direct Investment in the United States
by Major Industry and Country, End of 1967
(billions of dollars)

Area	Total	Manu-facturing	Finance and Insurance	Petroleum	Other
All Areas	9.9	4.2	2.2	1.9	1.7
Canada	2.6	1.4	.4	.1	.7
United Kingdom	3.2	1.0	1.2	.6	.3
Netherlands	1.5	.4	a	1.0	.1
Switzerland	1.1	.7	.3	––	a
Other Europe	1.2	.5	.2	.1	.4
Other Areas	.3	.1	.1	a	.1

aLess than $50 million.
Details may not add to totals due to rounding.
Source: U.S. Department of Commerce, *Survey of Current Business* (October, 1968).

TABLE 18

Capital Inflow and Reinvested Earnings
(millions of dollars)

	1965	1966	1967
Capital Inflow	57	86	251
Reinvested Earnings	357	339	440
Total	414	425	691

Source: U.S. Department of Commerce, *Survey of Current Business* (October, 1968).

TABLE 19

New Foreign Investments in the United States
(millions of dollars)

Country/Region	1965	1966	1967
Canada	58	25	19
United Kingdom	11	18	21
Belgium	1	——	——
France	2	3	2
Germany	14	36	37
Italy	3	1	2
Netherlands	——	3	a
Switzerland	6	a	34
Japan	2	3	18
Latin America	4	——	——
Other	——	a	a
Total	100	89	133

aLess than $500,000.
Details may not add to totals due to rounding.
Source: U.S. Department of Commerce, *Survey of Current Business* (September, 1967; October, 1968).

TABLE 20

Factors Affecting the Direct Foreign Investment Position
(millions of dollars)

	1965	1966	1967
Value, Beginning of Year	8,363	8,797	9,054
Capital Inflow			
New Investments	100	89	133
Other	−43	−3	118
Reinvested Earnings	357	339	440
Other Adjustments	20	−168	178
Value, End of Year	8,797	9,054	9,923

Details may not add to totals due to rounding.
Source: U.S. Department of Commerce, *Survey of Current Business* (October, 1968).

APPENDIX A

A recent sampling of manufacturing firms in the United States reveals that foreign control or beneficial interest is exercised in a number of ways, including affiliation, joint ventures, and new incorporation. The array of manufacturing enterprises owned or controlled by overseas entrepreneurs ranges from new, small- and medium-sized firms serving essentially local or regional markets to large, long-standing and heavily capitalized corporations which operate throughout the Continental United States and abroad.

INVESTING IN THE UNITED STATES—
FROM THE FOREIGN ENTREPRENEUR'S VIEWPOINT

Foreign firms investing in the United States gain immediate entry to one of the world's largest and most active markets. The value of goods and services produced annually in the United States now amounts to almost $900 billion, and the United States is in the midst of an unprecedented period of sustained economic expansion. The dynamic character of the U.S. economy arises from such diverse factors as the abundance of natural resources, the well-developed infrastructural base, the size and composition of the U.S. population, the geographic dimensions and topographic characteristics of the country, the income levels and spending habits of U.S. citizens, the size and structure of markets, and the inherent economies of sale of U.S. production.

While substantial numbers of foreign firms now export to the United States, foreign businessmen are becoming increasingly aware of the fact that manufacturing in the United States may often represent a more effective and remunerative means of serving U.S. markets. A number of key factors underlie the decision to shift from exporting to the U.S. market to manufacturing in the United States. Production *in* the United States *for* the United States, for example, eliminates many of the expenditures of time and money involved in export sales: special packing, marking, insurance, and transportation activities; additional shipping and financing documentation; wharfage and pierhandling outlays; tariffs and customs duties and clearance procedures; and warehousing necessities.

Manufacturing in the United States yields substantial marketing advantages: It facilitates, for example, immediate identification of and response to potential sales opportunities and permits more rapid adaptation of products to the changing tastes and demands of the U.S. buyer. Another major advantage is the opportunity for immediate access to the latest developments in U.S. research, management techniques, and production technology. In spite of generally higher prices, U.S. materials and production costs are lower for some industries.

Finally, the United States can serve as a base from which to supply overseas markets too distant to supply economically from the parent plant.

The assertion that investment in rather than export to the large U.S. market offers the prospect of greater profits but still leaves many firms in a quandry as to their potential for success in this vast market. For many firms, investment in the United States would clearly be neither advantageous nor advisable. However, many other firms might profitably take advantage of the potential for sound investment in the United States. For such firms, the United States offers the full array of resources and services needed for establishing a new enterprise. Financing, labor, raw materials, power, transportation, and other requisite resources are available in all parts of the nation. The availability of mobility of qualified managers and technicians means that new investors need bring very few key personnel to the United States. Furthermore, the United States has highly developed and adaptable advertising and distribution facilities for introducing new products to customers; a vast and efficient transportation system; and a broad range of advanced communication, data processing, and information-transmission systems to ease the tasks of management.

Investment in the United States, moreover, is eligible for the favorable federal tax treatment afforded new capital investment, for government programs to encourage investment in economically depressed regions of the United States, for the Small Business Administration's programs to help small- and medium-sized business, and for other federal government services which provide market information and contacts to prospective investors.

In addition, state and local governments, municipal and regional area-development authorities, industrial park authorities, chambers of commerce, local public utility companies, industrial realtors, banks, management-consultant firms, and transportation companies also provide a large variety of information services, and, in some instances, specific incentives for new investors.

Although recognizing the advantages outlined above, foreign businessmen may conclude that the U.S. market is too vast for small- and medium-sized foreign firms to compete in successfully. An even cursory investigation, however, reveals that the United States is actually a series of markets within markets. Thus, both foreign and domestic investors have found that they can produce and sell initially in one or more of the local or regional markets that comprise the total U.S. market. As sales grow and experience is gained, they can expand into other marketing areas.

In assessing his firm's potential for success, the foreign investor should be aware of the fact that small- and medium-sized firms are more typical of the U.S. business sector than the large U.S. corporations for which this country is so well known abroad. The significance of small- and medium-sized manufacturing firms is evident from the fact that of the 400,000 manufacturing business firms in the United States, over 96 per cent employ fewer than 250 workers, and these provide over 40 per cent of all manufacturing employment and produce more than 33 per cent of the value of all shipments. Another aspect of this question of size bears noting: Large and small firms are not forced to compete with each other. On the contrary, large firms are often a principal "market" for the products of smaller firms.

A frequently cited deterrent to investment in this country is the cost of producing in the United States, including particularly higher U.S. labor costs. While there is no doubt that U.S. workers are among the best paid in the world, their compensation is generally matched by their productivity and adaptability. Statistical data, moreover, lead to the conclusion that unit labor costs have risen faster abroad than in the United States. Nevertheless, U.S. labor costs are higher in most industrial sectors than they are abroad. Such costs, however, are only one element of total production. Other production inputs are quite often lower in the United States than abroad. On balance, total production costs for some products may therefore be lower in the United States than abroad.

LEGAL PROVISIONS AFFECTING FOREIGN INVESTMENT IN THE UNITED STATES

Foreign investors may not be informed of governmental regulations affecting business activity in this country. A few of the more important legal provisions are summarized below.

It is official U.S. Government policy to treat foreign capital essentially the same as domestic investment. With relatively minor exceptions, the foreign investor is free to use his capital in any way he wishes. The exceptions relevant to foreign firms involve a few sensitive activities in which foreign investment is restricted or regulated by federal law. These are almost exclusively outside the manufacturing sector and involve, for example, coastal shipping, domestic aviation, banking, hydroelectric-power generation, and leasing and mining of federal lands. Additional restrictions are imposed by a few states, but these are of little importance to potential foreign investors.

Although each state has its own incorporation and regulatory laws, differences among them are not substantial. Furthermore, once granted authority to operate in one state, a company is free to conduct business in all other states. In accordance with the principle of comity, the states generally follow a principle of equating companies organized in foreign countries with companies organized in other states of the United States.

Antitrust and related federal statues are, broadly speaking, intended to limit monopolistic actions which might result in restraint of trade, price discrimination, or misleading or deceptive business practices. Empirically, this legislation is directed primarily at larger business enterprises. The success of the many large corporations in the United States confirms the fact that antitrust regulations are neither unduly restrictive nor applied in an arbitrary or capricious manner. Moreover, the existence of these laws creates a climate receptive to and protective of new business ventures.

Firms from other countries will generally have no difficulty bringing their own management and technical staffs to the United States if a commercial treaty is in effect between the two countries. Such treaties exist between the United States and most industrialized nations. If there is no commercial treaty between the investor's country and the United States, it is more difficult to arrange entry for managerial and technical personnel. There are, however, a number of provisions in the U.S. Immigration Laws under which such personnel are permitted to enter and remain in the United States for limited periods.

U.S. Securities and Exchange Commission regulations are also of interest to potential foreign investors. The commission protects the general investing public against misrepresentation, manipulation, and other fraudulent practices in the purchase and sale of securities offered by a firm seeking to raise capital by issuing securities to the general public. The commission does not regulate access to the capital markets, nor does it pass on the merits of securities being offered to the public. Hence, in general, the commission represents no impediment to investment in the United States.

Of immediate concern to potential investors are U.S. tax laws. In regard to federal taxes, the Foreign Investment Tax Act of 1966 specifies that net income derived by resident foreign corporations from their U.S. operations is subject to the same tax rate as that for domestic corporations, i.e., 22 per cent on the first $25,000 of profit and 48 per cent on any amount above that figure. In addition, a temporary 10 per cent surcharge on corporate income taxes was adopted in 1968. Most states also levy income taxes on corporations located within their boundaries. Such taxes generally represent a fractional addition to federal taxes paid by corporations, and, in some cases, they may be reduced or eliminated, particularly during the initial years of business operation, under state programs to attract investment.

Treaties with most industrialized countries prevent double taxation and generally provide that taxes paid to the U.S. Government by a foreign-owned corporation can be credited against corresponding tax liabilities due the corporation's home goverment. Many of these treaties also provide preferential tax treatment for dividends, interest fees, and royalties earned in the United States by nonresident corporations. In certain instances, these treaties also provide for tax exemptions on one or more of these items.

Investment regulations designed to help improve the U.S. balance of payments were adopted in 1968. These relate to the flow of U.S. investment capital abroad and in no way depart from the long standing U.S. policy of unrestricted repatriation of capital and earnings to the parent company of the U.S. firm.

FOREIGN INVESTMENT IN THE UNITED STATES— FROM THE VIEWPOINT OF THE U.S. FIRM

Just as investment in the United States offers opportunities to foreign firms, U.S. firms can also benefit from this form of investment. In cases where foreign investors establish corporations without affiliation or association with U.S. firms, U.S. firms may secure a source of supply for better and less-costly products. Through contact with the techniques of the foreign entrepreneurs, they may also develop their own capabilities in similar lines. Furthermore, foreign firms in the United States acquire an appreciation of the circumstances involved in overseas operations that may affect favorably their judgment of the problems and operations of U.S. firms in their own countries.

Even greater potential advantages may accrue to U.S. firms participating in joint ventures, partnerships, or licensing arrangements with foreign investors. Through such direct contacts, diversification of product lines without associated development costs is possible; a strengthened financial position may result; and access to patents, designs, and processes owned by foreign companies may be acquired. Furthermore, competition from imported lines—possibly from the foreign partner's plant—may be displaced by domestic manufacture. Finally, the possibility of reciprocal licensing arrangements to distribute the U.S. firm's products in the foreign partner's sales territory, as well as the possibility of penetrating complementary markets and of expanding existing markets, is a significant potential benefit.

IMPACT ON THE U.S. ECONOMY

In a broader perspective and longer time frame, the United States can derive considerable benefit from the technology and new products developed abroad. Capital investment in the United States can introduce new products and perfect old ones, and it can increase U.S. productivity and add to domestic income and employment.

APPENDIX A

Foreign direct investment helps the U.S. balance of payments by increasing the flow of capital to the United States, by promoting domestic production of manufactured goods now being imported, and increasing U.S. exports over the longer term. Although investment from abroad generates payments of earnings abroad, the U.S. balance of payments should benefit in the longer term from greater productivity, import displacement, and export potential that flow from the investment of foreign capital.

THE "INVEST IN THE U.S.A." PROGRAM

An "Invest in the U.S.A." program was established by the U.S. Department of Commerce in 1961 in recognition of the benefits accruing from foreign direct investment to the United States. This program was included in the U.S. balance-of-payments program announced on January 1, 1968. The Invest in the U.S.A. Program provides a conduit and serves as an intermediary between U.S. firms and foreign investors in the promotion of joint ventures, licensing agreements, and other types of investment in the United States.

An industrial development attaché in Europe and U.S. commercial officers in key commercial centers abroad provide the overseas link for this program. These officials promote with potential overseas investors the specific investment and licensing proposals that have been formulated by U.S. firms and encourage overseas entrepreneurs to formulate investment and licensing proposals that can be disseminated to interested U.S. businessmen. The Commerce Department's field offices throughout the United States and its Washington staff in the Bureau of International Commerce provide the domestic link and perform the corollary work of seeking specific U.S. investment and licensing proposals for dissemination overseas and promoting in the U.S. business community proposals originating overseas.

B LIST OF FOREIGN FIRMS WITH SOME INTEREST OR CONTROL IN U.S. MANUFACTURING COMPANIES, JULY, 1969

This list of manufacturing companies in the United States which are subsidiaries or affiliates of foreign companies has been compiled from information contained in various public sources of business and corporate data and has not been verified with the companies listed. We have strived to list only "manufacturing" companies in the sense that each "makes" something or has an actual end product from its endeavor, though it be through pure manufacturing, oil-well drilling, newspaper printing, or a conversion process, while excluding from the list firms established for purposes of sales or services. Most of the U.S. companies listed are subsidiaries of foreign companies. The relationship of the companies reported as other than subsidiaries is indicated by one of the following abbreviations after the name of the company: A—affiliate, As—associate, I—investment, and JV—joint venture.

Location of Parent Company:

Australia

Australian Company	U.S. Company	Product
Kiwi Polish Co. Pty Ltd.	Kiwi Polish Company	Shoe polish
	Kiwi Coders Corporation	Marking equipment
Sandy Shaw Pty Ltd.	Sandy Shaw Inc.	Beach wear

Prepared by the U.S. Department of Commerce, Bureau of International Commerce

APPENDIX B

Belgium

Belgian Company

Bekaert S.A.	Bekaert Steel Wire Corp.	Steel wire drawing
Duesberg-Bosson S.A.	Duesberg-Bosson of America Inc.	Textile machinery
Blacieries de Saint-Roch S.A.	Franklin Glass Corp. 23.8% Virginia Glass Prod. 16.5%	Glassware
Petrofina, S.A.	American Petrofina Inc. American Petrofina Co. of Texas	Petroleum products
	American Liberty Pipe Line Company	Pipe
	Cos-Mar Inc. (JV with Marbon Division of Borg-Warner Corp.)	Petrochemicals
Solvay & Cie S.A.	Hedwin Corp. Baldwin Extruded Products Inc.	Plastic containers
Soudures Autogene S.A.	Arcos Corporation Arcwire Corporation Morgan Aluminum Welding Rod Company Arcflux Corporation	Welding equipment and related supplies
Tavernier, Robert	Erta, Inc.	Plastics
Usines Balteau S.A.	Balteau Electric Corp.	Industrial x-ray equipment

Canada

Canadian Company

Abitibi Paper Co. Ltd.	Abitibi Corporation	Pulp, newsprint, cartons wood paneling
Aerofall Mills Ltd.	Aerofall Mills Inc.	Ore-grinding mills
Alcan Aluminum Ltd.	Alcan Aluminum Corp. Alcan Metal Powders Inc. Alcan Cable Corp.	Aluminum, alloys, powders, fabrications

Canada (Continued)

Canadian Company

Algoma Steel Corp. Ltd.	Cannelton Coal Co.	Coal
	Fibron Limestone Co.	Stone
Allanson Mfg. Corp. Ltd.	Allanson Mfg. Corp.	Automotive equipment
Almex Automotive Ind., Div. of Vulcan Equipment Co., Ltd.	Vulcan Tire Inc.	Portable hoists, jacks
Anglo-Canadian Pulp & Paper Mills Ltd.	Anglo-Southern Paper Co.	Pulp and paper
Anthes Imperial Ltd.	Multiplex Company	Drink dispensing equipment
	Northeast Industries Inc.	
	John Wood Company	Pumps, heaters
Aqua-Marine Mfg. Ltd.	Aqua-Marine Inc.	Marine hardware
Atco Industries Ltd.	Northland Camps Inc.	Trailers
B & K Machinery Intl. Ltd.	B & K Machinery Inc.	Roll forming
Belding-Corticelli Ltd.	Butterfly Hosiery Co.	Women's finery
Blanchford, H. L. Ltd.	H. L. Blanchford, Inc.	Chemicals and wire-drawing compounds
Blast-Off Equipment Ltd.	Blast-Off International Corp.	Chemicals and chemical cleaning equipment
Blue Giant Equipment of Canada Ltd.	Blue Giant Equipment Corp.	Loading docks and ramps
Brace Ridge Lumber Co. Ltd.	Forgione Lumber Co.	Lumber
Bristol Aeroplane Co. of Canada Ltd.	Bristol Aeroplane Co. Inc.	Engines

Canada (Continued)

Canadian Company

CAE Industries Ltd.	Oneida Electronics Inc.	Electronic devices
Canada Iron Foundries Ltd.	Pacific Press & Shear Corp. Tamper Corporation	Hydraulic machinery
Canada Packers Ltd.	William Davies Co. Inc.	Meat processing
Canadian Breweries	Carling Brewing Co. (in 9 cities)	Breweries
	American Malting Co. (JV with Dominion Malting, Ontario, Ltd.)	Brewery ingredients
Canadian Liquid Air Ltd.	American Cryogenics, Inc.	Industrial gases and welding equipment
Canadian Marconi Co.	Kaar Electronics Corp. (in 6 cities)	Stereo phonos and communications equipment
Canadian Pearl Co. Ltd.	Elvee Manufacturing Co.	Imitation pearl necklaces
Canadian Wallpaper Manufacturers Ltd.	Birge Company, Inc. Handmark, Inc.	Wallpaper
Capitol Industries Ltd.	Capitol Industries Turret Electronics, Inc.	Furniture hardware TV tubes
Cargate Westminster Industries Ltd.	Cargate Company	Logging machinery
Carter Ltd., James B.	James B. Carter Inc.	Baseboard, unit and auto heaters
CCM, a Div. of Levy	CCM Inc.	Bicycles and skates
CEB Ltd.	CEB Corporation	Electric junction boxes
Century Fiberglass Ltd.	Century Fiberglass Inc.	Septic and water tanks

Canada (Continued)

Canadian Company

Chromium Mining and Smelting Corp. Ltd.	Chromium Mining & Smelting Corporation	Ferro alloys and ferro-silicon
Columbus McKinnon Ltd.	Columbus McKinnon Co.	Tire chains, hoists
Compagnie Pharmaco-Chimique, Inc.	Chemico-Pharmaceutical Co.	Deodorizers, cough syrup
Comstock Ltd. W. H.	Comstock Co.	Medicines
Combined Engineered Products Ltd. (formerly Turnbull Elevator of Canada Ltd.)	Turnbull Elevator Inc. Southeastern Elevator Seaberg Elevator Co. Frink Sno-Plows Co. Stuart Bros. Inc.	Elevators Elevators Elevators Snow-removal equipment Food preservatives
Consolidated Mining & Smelting Co. of Canada, Ltd. (Cominco Ltd.)	Cominco American Inc.	Fertilizer, metals
Consolidated Paper Corp. Ltd.	Consolidated Cellulose Products Inc. Doeskin Products Inc. APW Products Co. Ashland Paper Mills	Pulp, napkins, tissue, paper products
Craven Ltd.	Ovenaire Inc. (A) Filtaire Co. (A)	Crystal, ovens
Crush International Ltd.	Crush International Inc. Beverages International Inc. Inter-American-Orange-Crush Company	Soft drink formulating and bottling
Delta Electronics Ltd.	Kenmore Electronics Inc.	Amplifiers and signal-distribution equipment

Canada (Continued)

Canadian Company

Denison Mines Ltd.	Pacific Tin Consolidated Corp. (20%)	Tin mining
Diamond Clay Products Ltd.	Windsor Clay Products Empire Clay Products	Building material
Distillers Corp. Seagrams Ltd.	Joseph E. Seagram & Sons Inc. Browner Vintners Hunter-Wilson Paul Masson & Co.	Whiskies, wines, and other distilled beverages
Dominion Malting (Ontario) Ltd.	American Malting Inc. (JV with Canadian Breweries Ltd.)	Brewery ingredients
Dominion Textile Co. Ltd.	Industrial Speciality Mfg. Co. Howard Cotton Co.	Textile products
Domtar Ltd.	Domtar Chemicals Inc. Domtar Packaging Inc. Domtar Pulp & Paper Inc. Domtar Alabama Inc. Metal Powders Inc.	Chemicals, plastics, paper, pulp, powders
Duchon Bros. Signs Ltd.	Display Industries of America	Plastic signs
Dural Products Ltd.	Dural Products Co.	Adhesives
Dyment Ltd.	Dyment Co. (in 2 cities) Missouri Mounting & Finishing Co.	Mounters and finishers of window displays
Electrolyser Corp. Ltd.	Electrolyser Corp.	Electrolytic hydrogen and oxygen cells
Electronic Associates of Canada Ltd.	Electronic Automation Systems, Inc. Nuclear Radiation Developments Inc.	Sensors for measuring Paper industry Radioactive materials

Canada (Continued)

Canadian Company

Farris Brantford Ltd.	Farris Engineering Corp. (A)	Safety and relief valves
Fasco Controls Ltd.	Fasco Industries Inc. (As)	Oil-pressure switches
Ferritronics Ltd.	Ferritronics Inc.	Radio and electronic equipment
Fisher Gauge Works Ltd.	Fisher Gauge Works Inc.	Die-casting machinery
Foster Refrigerator of Canada Ltd.	Thermo Dynamics Inc.	Refrigeration
Fraser Companies Ltd.	Fraser Paper Co.	Wood pulp, paperboard
Foundation Co. of Canada Ltd.	Atlantic Tug & Equipment Corp.	Construction equipment
Fulford Ltd., G. T.	W. T. Hanson Corp.	Medicines
General Woods and Veneers Ltd.	Swords Veneer & Lumber Co.	Hardwood veneers
General Impact Extrusions	General Impact Extrusions	Aluminum tubes
Grand Anse Peat Moss Ltd.	Grand Anse Peat Moss Co.	Process peat moss
Greey Mixing Equipment Ltd.	Mixing Equipment Co. Inc. (As)	Fluid mixers and agitators
Haines Manufacturing Co. Ltd.	Haines Manufacturing Co. (in 2 cities)	Potato grading and handling equipment
Hawker Siddeley Canada Ltd.	Orenda Inc.	Gas turbine engines
Heede Canada Ltd., B. M.	B. M. Heede (Calif.) Inc.	Climbing cranes and hoists

Canada (Continued)

Canadian Company

Herzog Enterprises Ltd.	Pacific Ropes Inc.	Braided nylon ropes
Hooper & Co. Ltd., S. W.	S. W. Hooper Corp.	Pulp and paper-mill equipment
Husky Oil Ltd.	Husky Oil Company Bristol Bay Oil Co. International Oil & Gas Corp.	Petroleum, natural gas, petroleum byprod- ucts
	Gate City Steel Corp.	Steel
	Marsh Steel and Aluminum Co.	Steel and aluminum
	Rum River Charcoal Co. Husky Briquetting Inc. Curtis Inc. (I) (33.3%)	Carbon utilization
Industrial Minerals of Canada Ltd.	American Nepheline Corp.	Raw material for glass
International Bronze Powder Ltd.	United States Bronze Powders, Inc.	Bronze and aluminum powders
International Nickel Co. of Canada Ltd.	International Nickel Co., Inc. (rolling mill in 1 state, research labs in 3 states)	Nickel research, mining, and conversion
Kardar Canadian Oil Ltd.	Kardar American Oils Inc.	Oil exploration and production
Kaumagraph Ltd.	Kaumagraph Company	Lithographed fabric labels
Kindred Industries Ltd.	Ziegler Harris Corp.	Stainless steel sinks
Labatt (John) Ltd.	General Brewing Co.	Breweries
Lamb Industries of Canada Ltd.	White Products Corp. (As)	Water Heaters, alumi- num combo doors and windows

Canada (Continued)

Canadian Company

Leigh Instruments Ltd.	Leigh Systems Inc.	Navigational and aeronautical instruments
London & Petrolia Barrel Co., Ltd.	General Cooperage Inc.	Barrels, wheels, and rims
MacDowell Brothers Ltd.	MacDowell Brothers Co.	Breakfast foods, flours, specialties
MacLean-Hunter Publishing Co., Ltd.	MacLean-Hunter Publishing Corporation	Publisher of magazines, directories
MacMillan Bloedel Ltd.	Blanchard Lumber Co.	Wood
	MacMillan Bloedel Products Inc. (plants in 3 cities)	Corrugated cartons; paperboard
	MacMillan Bloedel United Inc. (60%) (JV with United Fruit Co. holding other 40%)	Paper mill
Massey-Ferguson Ltd.	Massey-Ferguson Inc.	Farm, industrial equipment
	Perkins Engines Co.	Engines
Maknur Laboratories Ltd.	ALCAM Scientific Co.	Instruments for testing chlorine in water
Mimik Ltd.	DeSilvey Corp.	Hydraulic devices
Modenco Ltd.	Modenco Corp. (in 2 cities)	Electrical components
Molson Breweries Ltd.	Sicks-Rainier	Brewery
Moore Corp. Ltd.	Moore Business Forms Inc.	Printer of business forms
	F. N. Burt Company	Paper boxes
	Kidder Press Company	Printing presses
	Stacy Machine Company	Machinery

Canadian Company

Morse Corp. Ltd., Robert	Howe Richardson Scale Co.	Scales
	Johnston Pump Company	Pumps
Niagara Terrazzo Supplies Ltd.	American Terrazzo Strip Inc.	Terrazzo (mosaic flooring) strips
Niagara Wire Weaving Co., Ltd.	Canada Niagara Wire Weaving Company Southern Wires Inc.	Fine mesh wire screens
Noranda Mines Ltd.	Wolverine Die Cast	Power presses, piercing and notching machines
Plastiglide Ltd.	Plastiglide Manufacturing Corp.	Furniture hardware
Perma-Flex Industries Ltd.	Perma-Flex Roller Corp.	Printing-rollers and covers
Richardson Mfg. Ltd.	Richardson Mfg. Corp.	Auto bug and gravel guards
Rio Algom Mines Ltd.	Rio Algom Corp.	Mineral mining
Rotaflex of Canada, Ltd.	"R" Manufacturing Co.	Cellulose acetate luminaires
Salada Foods, Ltd.	Plant Industries, Inc.	Food products
Scintrex Ltd.	Scintrex Inc.	Stereophonic headphones
	Mineral Surveys Inc.	Mineral exploration
	Scintrex Airborne Geophysics Inc.	Airborne geophysical services
Seven Arts Productions Ltd.	Warner Brothers Pictures Inc.	Film production
	REA Express Seven Arts Transvision Inc. (JV with REA Express)	Visual entertainments

Canada (Continued)

Canadian Company

Sheldons Engineering Ltd.	Sheldons Mfg. Corp.	Fans, blowers
Sicard Inc. Ltd.	Sicard Industries Inc.	Snow plows, sweepers
Sinclair Radio Laboratories Ltd.	Sinclair Radio Laboratories Inc.	Radio and electronic equipment
Sirco Products Ltd.	Sirco Controls Co.	Electric and pneumatic control switches
Stuart Bros. Ltd.	Stuart Flavors Inc.	Flavoring extracts and concentrates
Supersign Co. Ltd.	Aluminum & Plastic Sign Mfg. Co.	Directories, bulletin boards, and signs
Superpack Vending Ltd.	Scientific Packaging Corp.	Vending machines
Sutherland Press Ltd.	Thomas D. Murphy Co.	Printer of calendars
Sweeney Coopeage Ltd.	Sweeney Coopeage Inc.	Barrels
Thomson Newspapers Ltd.	Thomson Newspapers Inc. Brush-Moore Newspapers Inc.	Publishers of 34 daily and 11 weekly newspapers
Velan Engineering Ltd.	Velan Steam Specialties (A)	Thermostatic steam traps, mono- and forged-steel valves
Vickers Krebs Ltd.	Vickers Krebs Inc.	Chemical apparatus, stills
Walker (Hiram) & Sons Ltd.	Hiram Walker & Sons W. A. Taylor & Co., Inc.	Elevators Elevators
Walker (Hiram)-Gooderham & Worts Ltd.	Riverside Elevator Co.	Elevators

Canada (Continued)

Canadian Company

Weston (George) Ltd.	Loblaw Inc. (64.2%) National Tea Co. (52.5%) (1000 food stores) Weston Biscuit Co. American-Superior Biscuit Co. Southern Biscuit Co.	Food products

Denmark

Danish Company

Burmeister & Wain's Maskin-Og Skibsbyggeri	Burmeister & Wain American Corp.	Shipbuilding
Chr Hansen's Laboratorium	Hansen's Chemistry Laboratory Inc.	Preparations for the dairy industry
Smidth & Co. AS, F. L.	F. L. Smidth & Co.	Heavy machinery
Haldor Topsoe	Haldor Topsoe, Inc.	Catalysts for chemical industry
NOPI AS	Nopitape Inc.	Tape Products

England

British Company

Addison Electric	Addision Electric Co. Inc.	Instrumentation for cable makers
Albright & Wilson Ltd.	W. J. Bush & Co. Bush Boake Allen Inc.	Industrial chemicals
Alexander Alec, Ltd.	Lortogs Inc.	Children's sportswear
Associated Motor Cycles Ltd.	The Indian Co.	Motorcycles and engines

England (Continued)

British Company

Babcock & Wilcox Ltd.	Babcock & Wilcox Co.	Boilers, refractories
Baker Perkins Ltd.	Baker Perkins Inc.	Bakery equipment
Barrow, Hepburn & Gale Ltd.	Colloids Inc.	Specialty chemicals
Beecham Group Ltd.	Beecham Research Labs	Cosmetics, toiletries, drugs
Birfield Ltd.	Bound Brook Bearing Corp.	Bearings and valves
Birmingham Sound Reproducers Ltd.	Discus Corp.	Electronic devices
Borax Ltd.	United States Borax & Chemical Corp. (73%) U.S. Borax Research Corp. U.S. Potash (30%)	Boron produces and chemicals Potassium
Bowater Paper Corp.	Bowaters United States Corp. Bowaters Carolina Corp. Bowaters Southern Paper Catawba Newsprint Co. (JV with Newhouse Newspaper Group)	Sulphate, pulp newsprint, paper Paper for 21 daily newspapers
‚Bradford Dyers' Assn. Ltd.	Bradford Dyeing Assn.	Textile processor
British Nylor Spinners Ltd.	Fiber Industries Inc. (12%) Nylon Industries Inc. (12%)	Synthetic fibers
British-American Tobacco Co. Ltd.	Brown & Williamson Tobacco Corp. Vita Food Products Inc.	Tobacco products Food products
British Paints (Holdings) Ltd.	Federal Paint Co. Inc.	Paint

England (Continued)

British Company

British Petroleum Company Ltd. (BP)	BP Exploration Co. (Alaska) Inc. BP Exploration U.S.A. Inc. (formerly Kern Oil) St. Helens Petroleum Corp. BP Explorations (JV with Sinclair Oil Corp.) Sinclair Gas Stations (10,000)	Petroleum exploration and production
British Ropes Ltd.	British Ropes Corp. International Ropes Inc. (I)	Ropes, twines, chains
Brockhouse & Co. Ltd.	Brockhouse Corp. Donnelly Mfg. Co.	Engineering products
Brook Motors Ltd.	Brook Motor Corp.	Electric motors
Brown, David Ltd.	Foote Brothers	Transmission equipment and gears
Burmah Oil Company	Southdown Burmah Oil (60%) (JV w/Southdown Inc.–40%)	Petroleum
Caravans International Ltd.	Caravan International Corp.	Trailers
Cole, E. K. Ltd.	American Tradair Corp.	Electronic products
Consolidated Gold Fields Ltd.	American Zinc, Lead & Smelting Co. Buell Engineering Co., Inc. Tri-State Zinc Inc.	Metal and mineral mining Industrial cleaning machines
Cooper, McDougall & Robertson Ltd.	Cooper & Nephews Inc.	Veterinary chemicals

England (Continued)

British Company

Courtaulds Ltd.	Courtaulds North America, Inc.	Synthetic fibers
	Red Wand Compositions, Inc.	Marine paint
De LaRue International Ltd., Thos.	De LaRue Inc.	Printing
Dick Ltd., R & J	R & J Dick Co., Inc.	Belt power transmission
Dunlop Rubber Co. Ltd.	Dunlop Tire & Rubber Corp.	Tires, tubes, sports equipment
Dexion Ltd.	Dexion, Inc.	Steel pallet racks and shelving material
Du Pont Ltd.	Ewarts-Baldwin Forgings Co. Inc.	Iron, steel
ECL Industries Ltd.	Mechanical Products Inc.	Circuit breakers
Edwards High Vacuum (International)	Edwards High Vacuum Inc. Getters Electronics Inc.	High vacuum pumps, vacuum-measuring instruments and control devices
EMI Ltd. (Electrical & Musical Industries)	Capitol Records Morphy-Richards Inc.	Recordation, electronics
English Electric Co. Ltd.	English Electric Corp.	Electrical equipment
English Sewing Cotton Co. Ltd.	American Thread Co.	Yarn and thread
Everett & Co. Ltd.	Everett Products Inc.	Surgical equipment
Ferranti Ltd.	Ferranti Electric Inc.	Transformers, meters
Fielden Electronics Ltd.	Control Electronics Inc.	Electronic devices

England (Continued)

British Company

Fisons Ltd.	Fisons Corporation
	  Patco Inc.
	  Lee Patten Seed Co.
	Albatross Fertilizers, Inc.
	  (50%)
	National Polychemicals, Inc.
	Doggett-Fison (80%)
		Organic chemicals, fert-
		ilizers, seeds, garden-
		ing material

Foseco Ltd.	Foseco Inc.	Metal-treatment equip- ment
General Electric Co. of Great Britain-Associ- ated Electrical Indus- tries Ltd.	AEI Liaison Services Ltd. Eugene Munsell & Co.	Mica electronic compo- nents
Gestetner Ltd.	Gestetner Corp.	Duplicating machines
Guest Keen and Nettle- folds Ltd.	General Swedish Hardware Corp. (86.1%)	Building supplies and engineering equip- ment
HP Sauce Ltd.	Lea & Perrins Inc.	Food products
Horlicks Ltd.	Horlicks Corp.	Malted-milk products
Hope Ltd., Henry & Sons	Hope's Windows Inc.	Windows, metal

Imperial Chemical In-
dustries Ltd.
	ICI (Organics), Inc.
	Chemical Mfg. Co., Inc.
	Fiber Industries Inc. (37%)
	  Hylon Industries Inc.
	Katalco (JV with Nalco C
	  Chemical Co.)
	Rubicon Chemicals (JV
	  with U.S. Rubber Corp.)
		Chemicals, pharmaceu-
		ticals, synthetic
		fibers, and dyes
		
		Catalysts

Imperial Tobacco Co. Ltd.	Imperial Tobacco Co. Uddo & Taormina Corp.	Leaf tobacco Canned and frozen foods

England (Continued)

British Company

Inertia Switch Ltd.	Inertia Switch Inc. (A)	Acceleration switches
International Paints (Holdings) Ltd.	International Paint Co.	Surface coatings
International Publishing Corp. Ltd.	Cahners Publishing Co. Inc. (I) (40%) Canover-Mast Publications Inc.	Publisher of business journals
Inveresk Paper Company Ltd.	Inveresk Paper Corp. Louisiana Forest Products Corp. (JV with Riegel Paper Co.)	Paper, paperboard pulp
J & J Cash Ltd.	J & J Cash Inc.	Woven labels
J & P Coats Ltd.	Coats & Clark Inc.	Threads
Johnson, Matthey & Company Ltd.	Johnson, Matthey & Co. Inc. J. Bishop & Co., Platinum Works	Refiners of metals
Jute Industries Ltd.	Stanley Belting Corp. Jute Industries Ltd. of New York Inc.	Textiles and jute products
Lansing Bagnall Ltd.	Lansing Towmotor Inc. (JV with Towmotor Corp., a subsidiary of Caterpillar)	Materials-handling equipment
Lister & Co. Ltd.	Lister-Blackstone Inc.	Diesel engines
MacMillan & Co. Ltd.	St. Martin's Press Inc.	Publisher
Megator Pumps & Compressors Ltd.	Megator Corp.	Pumps
Midland Tar Distillers Ltd.	Midland Tar Distillers Inc.	Tar products

England (Continued)

British Company

Monotype Corp. Ltd.	Lanston Industries Inc. (As)	Office equipment
Moorwood-Vulcan Ltd.	Vulcan-Hart Corp. (As)	Commercial cooking equipment
Morgan Crucible Co. Ltd.	Morganite Inc. Whittaker-Morgan (40%) (JV with Whittaker Corp.)	Electrical and refractory products Carbon-fiber materials
Muirhead & Co. Ltd.	Muirhead Instruments Inc.	Electronic parts
Neill & Co. (Sheffield) Ltd., James	James Neill & Co.	Hacksaw blades, tools
Norcross Ltd.	Spencer Corp., J. P.	Dry cleaning and coin-op machinery
Parmelee (CB) Ltd.	United States Safety Service Co.	Eye and face protection equipment
Penich & Ford Ltd.	Bacon Products Corp.	Bacon-rinds processing
Penguin Books Ltd.	Penguin Books Inc.	Publisher
Permali Ltd.	Permali Inc.	Industrial laminates
Photo-Me International Ltd.	Auto-Photo Co.	Coil-operated photographic machines
Plessey Dynamics	Plessey Airborne Inc.	Aircraft parts
Powell Duffryn Group	Name unknown (JV with American Hoist & Derrick Co.)	Hydraulic machinery
Rawlplug Co. Ltd.	Rawlplug Co., Inc.	Masonry drilling tools
Racal Electronics Ltd.	Racal Communications Inc.	Electronic equipment

England (Continued)

British Company

Reckitt & Colman Holdings Inc. Ltd.	L. C. Forman & Sons Inc.	Food products
	R. T. French Co.	Food products
	Widmer's Wine Cellars Inc. (I)	Wine
Redland Group	Pismo Safety Corp.	Highway signs and markings
	Wald Industries Inc.	
Reed Paper Group Ltd.	Anglo-Southern Paper Corp. (96%)	Pulp and paperboard, and paper products
	Birge Co., Inc. (65%)	
	W. H. S. Lloyd Co., Inc.	
	Montmorency Paper Co. Inc. (96%)	
	J. H. Thorp & Co. Inc.	
Rio Tinto-Zinc Corporation Ltd.	Pyrites Co. Inc.	Cobalt and copper
	Yttrium Corp. of Amerca (JV with Molybdenum Corp. of America) (49%)	Yttrium oxide
	Alloys and Chemicals Corp.	Aluminum smelting
	I. Schumann Co.	Aluminum and zinc alloys
	Reco Chemicals Inc. (50%)	
Robinson Ltd.	Ascot Chemicals and Adhesives Co.	Adhesives
Schermuly Ltd.	Smith and Wesson Pyrotechnics Inc. (JV with Smith and Wesson, Inc.)	Line throwing equipment, distress signals, and markers
Sears Holding Ltd.	Sears Industries Inc. (62%)	Laundry service
	Consolidated Laundries Corp.	
	Tiffany Textiles Inc.	Knitwear
Shaw Petrie Ltd.	Clyde Tube Forgings	Forgings

England (Continued)

British Company

Selection Trust Ltd.	American Metal Climax (11.8%)	Nonferrous metals
Shell Transport & Trading Co., Ltd. Shell Petroleum Ltd.[1]	Shell Oil Company (27.8%) Shell Chemicals Co.	Petroleum Chemicals
Staveley Machine Tools Ltd.	Lapointe Machine Tool Co.	Machine tools
Steel & Co. Ltd.	Coles Cranes Inc.	Mobile cranes and lifting magnets
Thermal Syndicate Ltd.	Thermal American Fused Quartz Co.	Fused-quartz silica
Thermotank Ltd.	Thermotank Inc.	Containers
Tunnel Portland Cement Company Ltd.	National Portland Cement Co. Ryan Ready Mixed Concrete Corp.	Construction materials
Turner & Newall Corp.	Certain-Teed Products Corp. (15%)	Millwork and pipes
Unilever Organization Unilever Ltd.[2]	Lever Brothers T. J. Pipton Co. Good Humor Ice Cream Co. Pennsylvania Dutch Megs Wishbone Products	Soaps and oils Food products Frozen dairy products Macaroni Salad dressings

---

[1]Shell Transport & Trading Co., Ltd. and Royal Dutch Petroleum Co. of the Netherlands are holding companies with 40 per cent and 60 per cent interest, respectively, in the Royal Dutch/Shell Group, which consists of Shell Petroleum, and Bataafse Petroleum Maatschapij N.V. and their subsidiaries.

[2]Unilever Ltd. and Unilever N.V. of the Netherlands are holding companies which constitute the Worldwide Unilever Organization. Although the U.S. firms listed above may be assigned to Unilever N.V., the two parent companies (N.V. and Ltd.) have an agreement providing for an equal distribution of dividends and earnings.

APPENDIX B

England (Continued)

British Company

Vanesta Ltd.	Arkwright-Interlaken Inc.	Bookcloth and tracing
Vavasseur & Co. Ltd.	Wood & Selick Coconut Co. Inc.	Food products
Vickers Ltd.	Vickers-Armstrongs Inc. Vickers-Instruments Inc. Racine and Vickers Armstrongs Inc.	Shipbuilding, pumps, valves, controls
Vickers McKay Ltd.	McKay Machine Co.	Sheet- and strip-mill equipment
Viyella International Ltd.	Solly Allen Ltd.	Textile products
Wellcome Foundation Ltd.	Burrough Wellcome & Co. (USA) Inc.	Pharmaceuticals and chemicals
Winsor & Newton Ltd.	Winsor & Newton Inc.	Artists' colors
Yardley & Co. Ltd.	Yardley of London Inc.	Perfumes, soaps

Finland

Finnish Company

OY Tam Pella AB	Pineville Kraft Corp.	Kraftliner

France

French Company

Air Liquide Co.	American Cryogenics, Inc.	Industrial gases and welding equipment
Antargaz (subsidiary of Antar Petroles de l'Atlantique)	Solarconics, Inc. (JV with Southern Industries)	Infrared heating unit
BIC S.A.	Waterman BIC Pen Co., Inc.	Writing instruments

France (Continued)

French Company

Carbone Lorraine	Carbone Corp.	Brushes, batteries
Compagnie de Saint-Gabain	American-Saint Gobain Corp. (57%) Franklin Glass Corp. Certain Teed Saint-Gobain Insulation Corp. (affiliated with Certain-Teed Products Corp.)	Glass and fiber glass
Compagnie Française des Petroles	Leonard Refineries (33.3%)	Petroleum refining
Compagnie Generale de Geophysique	Georex Inc. (USA)	Oil and mineral exploration
Compagnie Generale de Telegraphie San Fils	Intercontinental Electronics Co. Warnecke Electron Tubes, Inc. (JV with Hallicrafters; CSF owns 58%) American Radio Co.	Electric equipment and parts A shell for licensing and cross-licensing arrangements
Compagnie Industrielle	Cable Communications Systems, Inc. (JV with Simplex Wire & Cable Co.)	Cable systems
Comptoir de Industrie Contonniere	Christian Dior-New York Inc.	Dresses, coats, and blouses
Degremont Co.	Degremont Inc. (30%) Degremont-Cottrell (JV with Research-Cottrell, Inc.)	Water- and waste-treatment equipment
Dollfus-Mieg & Cie S.A.	DMC Corp.	Fiber spinners

France

French Company

Nadella, S.A.	Garlock-Nadella Inc. (JV with Garlock Inc. having majority interest)	Needle bearings
Pechiney Compagnie de Products Chimiques et Electrometalur-giques	Howmet Corp. (46%)	Aluminum and steel products
	Firth-Loach Metals Inc.	Carbide products,
	Intalco Aluminum Corp. (JV with American Metal Climax. Pechiney and Howmet each own 25%)	aluminum production
Pont-a-Mousson (and its subsidiary, HITMA)	Glamorgan Pipe & Foundry (59%)	Plastic and metal pipes
	Glan Weiskettel Pipe & Foundry Co.	
Rhone-Poulenc S.A.	Rhodia Inc.	Weed killers, synthetic fibers
	Chipman Chemical Co.	
	Phillips Fibers Corp. (JV with Phillips Petroleum Co.)	
Roger & Gallet	Concentrate Mfg. Co.	Concentrates
Roussel Uclaf S.A.	Roussel Corp.	Pharmaceutical special-ties
Regis Autonome des Petroles, and Soci-ete Nationale des Petroles d'Aquitaine	Oil Shale Corp.	Petroleum and petrole-um byproducts
	Auxirap Corp. of America	
	Acquitane Oil Corp.	
	Aquitaine-Organico	Chemicals
Societé le Nickel	Kaiser Nickel Co. (JV with Kaiser Aluminum and Chemical Corp.)	Ferronickel
Societé Financiere de Transport Et d'En-terprises	Brown Drilling Co.	Oil-well drilling

West Germany

West German Company

AG Kugel Fischer Georg Schafer	Norma AG Bearing Corp.	Ball and roller bearings
Artos Machinen	American Artos	Textile machinery
Badische Anilin- & Soda-Fabrik AG (BASF)	BASF Corporation	Dyes and other chemicals
	Carlstadt Leather Finishes Co.	Dyestuffs and tanning chemicals
	United Cork Co.	Cork
	Computron, Inc.	Magnetic tape
	Dow-Badische Chemicals, Inc. (JV with Dow Chemical)	Synthetic fibers
Barmer Maschinenfabrik AG	American Barmag Corp.	Textile and fiber machines
Bayer (Fabenfabriken) AG	FBA Pharmaceuticals Inc.	Pharmaceuticals
	Chemagro Corp.	Chemicals: insecticides, defoliants, synthetic materials and fibers
	Mobay Chemical Co.	
	Hearmann & Riemer Corp.	
	Verona-Pharma Chemical Corp.	
	Vero Beach Laboratories	
Boehler & Weber AG	American Permac Inc.	Dry cleaning and textile-finishing machines
Bosch BmbH	American Bosch Arma Corp.	Electronic and electrical equipment
	Bacharach Industrial Instrument Co.	Mechanical, chemical, and electrical measuring instruments
	Lepco, Inc.	
Brueckner Trockentechnik AG	Bruckner Machinery Corp.	Textile machinery
BYK-GULDEN Lomberg KG	BYK-GULDEN Inc.	Pharmaceuticals, chemicals

APPENDIX B

West Germany

West German Company

Cassella Farbwerke Mainkur AG	Sou-Tex Chemical Co. Inc. (63%)	Petrochemicals and dyestuffs
Collo-Rheincollodium GmbH	American Collo Corp.	Foam panels
Degussa GmbH	Celastic Corp. Electric Thermometers, Inc. (50%)	Chemicals Electric thermometers
Dragoco Gerberding	Dragoco Inc.	Flavors, fragrances
Dynamit Nobel	Rubber Corp. of America (35%)	Plastics
Feinpapierfabrik Felix Schoeller	Schoeller Technical Papers Inc. (JV with Simpson Lee Paper Co.)	Photographic and technical papers
Felten & Guilleaume Carlswerk AG	Felton & Guilleaume Products Corp. (60%) United States Cable Corp. (33.3%)	Metal products
Freudenberg, Carl	Pellon Corp. Disogrin Industries	Nonwoven fabrics Polyurethane oil seals
Gebrueder Heller	American Heller Corp. (50%)	Deep-hole boring equipment
Haarmann & Reimer GmbH	Haarmann & Reimer Corp.	Aromatics, perfume
Hamac-Hansella Machinen	Hamac-Hansella Machine Corp.	Candy-mixing machinery
Hazemag Hartzerkleinerungs-und Zement-Maschinenbau GmbH	Hazemag USA Inc.	Crushing machinery
Hengstler, J., KG	Hecon Corp.	Counting devices and systems

West Germany (Continued)

West German Company

Henkel & Cie GmbH	Standard Chemical Products Inc.	Textile auxiliaries, cosmetic and detergent intermediates
Herberts & Co., Dr. Kurts	American Herberts Corp.	Laminating adhesives
Herder, Verlag	Herder & Herder Inc.	Books and periodicals
Hoechst (Farbwerke)	American Hoechst Corp.	
	Carbic-Hoechst Corp.	Dyestuffs
	Hostachem Corp.	Chemicals
	Hostawax Co.	Waxes
	Hoechst Pharmaceutical Co.	Pharmaceuticals
	National Laboratories Corp.	Veterinary biologics
	Azoplate Corp. (85%)	Presensitized offset plates
	Stauffer Hoechst Polymer Corp. (JV with Stauffer Chemical Co.)	Chemicals
	Hystron Fibres Inc. (JV with Hercules Inc.)	Synthetic fibers
	Gulf Central Pipeline Co. (JV with Mannesmann AG, Thyssen AG, Santa Fe RR, Gulf Interstate Engr. Co.)	Liquified anhydrous ammonia pipeline from New Orleans to the Midwest
Ilseder Hutte	American Pecco Corp.	Construction equipment
	Delta Steel Inc.	Iron, coal, and steel
Industrie-Companie Kleinewerfers Konstruktions-und Handelsges mbH	Thermal Transfer Corp. (73%)	Heat exchangers
Kloeckner-Humboltd-Deutz AG	Deutz Diesel Corp.	Engines, trucks, mining machinery

West Germany (Continued)

West German Company

KORF Industrie-und Handel GmgH	Trans-American Steel Corp.	Wire and springs
Krautkramer, Dr. J.	Krautkramer Ultrasonics Inc.	Ultrasonic equipment
Kuhnke, Elektrotechnische Fabrik GmbH	L. Kuhnke, Inc.	Electrical equipment
Kuhlmann, Franz KG	Kuhlmann-Impex Inc.	Drafting and office equipment, grinders
Mannesmann AG	Easton Metal Powder Co., Co., Inc.	Plastics
	Mannesmann-Meer Inc.	Steel processing
	Concast Inc. (JV with Concast AG, Switzerland, and National Steel Corp.)	Steel
	Gulf Central Pipeline Co. (JV with Hoechst, Farbwerke, Thyssen AG, Santa Fe RR, Gulf Interstate Engineering Co.)	Liquified anhydrous ammonia pipeline from New Orleans to the Midwest
Melitta Werke Bentz & Sohn	Melitta Inc.	Coffeemakers
Moehring Enterprises	Atlantic Veneer	Veneer
Persil	Standard Chemical Products Inc.	Chemicals
Piel & Adey	Piad Precision Casting Corp. (50%)	Nonferrous permanent mold casting
Rehau Plastiks GmbH	Rehau-Plastiks Inc.	Plastic extrusions, moldings
Ringsdorf-Werke GmbH	Ringsdorf Corp. (50%)	Electrical components

West Germany (Continued)

West German Company

Rothe Erde-Schmiedig AG	Rotek Inc. (50%)	Antifriction bearings
Salzdetfurth AG	Chemsalt, Inc.	Potash and sodium sulphate
Schott und Gen, Jenaer Glaswerk	Schott Optical Glass Inc.	Optical glass
Siemens AG	Stromberg-Carlson Corp. (11.5%)	Electronics and electrical equipment
	U.S. Instruments Inc. (I)	Phone equipment
Soehne, Johann Kleine-werfers AG	Beloit-Kleinewerfers Textile Machinery Corp. (JV with Beloit Industries)	Textile machinery
Springer-Verlag GmbH	Springer-Verlag New York Inc.	Books
Stinnes AG, Hugo	American Drill Bushing Co. Richard Brothers Punch Co. Welch Tool Sales, Inc.	Drill bushings, components, dies, tool components
Telefonbau & Normal-zeit GmbH	Tele-Norm Corp. Postalia Corp.	Telecommunications equipment, postage-meter equipment
Textile-Maschinen-Fabrik	Mayer American Textiles Machines Inc.	Warp-knitting machinery and accessories
Thyssen AG	Gulf Central Pipeline Co. (JV with Hoechst, Farb-werke, Mannesmann AG, Santa Fe RR, Gulf Interstate Engineering Co.)	Liquified anhydrous ammonia pipeline from New Orleans to the Midwest
Vereinigte Aluminum-Werk AG	VAW United Aluminum Works of America Inc.	Aluminum billets and tubes
	Channel Master Corp.	Aluminum tubes

West Germany (Continued)

West German Company

Wacker-Chemie GmbH	Wacker Chemical Corp.	Semiconductor materials
Worms Renolit Werke GmbH	American Renolit Corp.	Plastic sheets

Italy

Italian Company

Buitoni	Buitoni Foods Corp.	Food product
Fasco AG (a part of the Michele Sindona Industrial Organization)	Oxford Electric	Electrical equipment
Montecatini Edison SpA	Novamont, Inc.	Chemicals
OCRIM SpA	Mississippi Grain Co. Mid-South Flour & Feed Mills Inc.	Grain Mills
Olivetti	Olivetti-Underwood	Office equipment

Japan

Japanese Company

Alaska Pulp Co., Ltd.	Alaska Lumber & Pulp Co., Inc. Wrangell Lumber Co.	Pulp and lumber
Iwakura-Gumi Lumber Co.	South Central Timber Development Inc.	Lumber
Japan Gas Chemical	Collier Carbon & Chemical (JV with Japan Gas Chemical)	Urea fertilizer plant
Matsushita Electric Industrial Co., Ltd.	Matsushita Electric of Puerto Rico, Inc. Matsushita Electric Corp. of America	Radios and electrical equipment

Japan (Continued)

Japanese Company

Matsutoyo Mfg., Ltd.	Sampou Mfg., Inc.	Micrometers
Mitsubishi Shoji Kaisha Ltd. (20%) Nichiro Gyogyo Kaisha Ltd. (30%)	Orca Pacific Packing Co. (JV with New England Fish Company)	Seafood processing and packing
OJI Lumber Co. (Subsidiary of OJI Paper Co.) Sogo Boeki Kaisha Ltd.	Alaska Prince Timber Co. (51%)	Sawmill
Okura Trading Co. Ltd. Danto Co. Ltd.	Marmoles of Puerto Rico, Inc.	Ceramic tile
Taiyo Fishery Co., Ltd.	Maryland Tuna Corp. (40%; other 60% owned by Bumble Bee Seafoods Inc., Div. of Castle & Cooke Inc.) B and B Fish Inc. Pacific Alaska Fisheries Co. (49%)	Seafood processing and packaging
	Western Alaska Enterprises (51% by Peter Pan Fisheries Inc.)	Roe processing
Teikoku Oil Ltd.	Alaska Petroleum Resources Co. (Alaskco)	Petroleum
Tsuzuki Spinning Co. Ltd.	Henderson Mills Inc.	Automated spinning and weaving equipment
Yokogawa Electric Works Ltd.	Acrohm Electronic Co.	Indicating instruments
Yoshida Kogyo K. K. Yoshida Shoji Co., Ltd.	Yoshida International Co.	Slide fasteners, fastener-making machines

Netherlands

Dutch Company

Albatros Superfosfaat- fabrieken N.V.	Albatros Fertilizers Inc. (50%, other 50% owned by Fisons Ltd., England)	Garden products
Algemeene Norit Maatschappij N.V.	American Norit Co., Inc.	Activated carbon
Algemene Kunstzijde Unie N.V. (AKU)	American Enka Corp. (56%)	Synthetic fibers
Bataafse Petroleum Maatschappij N.V. (BPM)[3]	Shell Oil Company (69.4%) Shell Chemical Co.	Petroleum Chemicals
Buehrmann-Tetterode N.V.	G. H. Buhrman Inc.	Printing
Chenische Fabriek N.V.	Naarden Flavorex Co.	Flavorings
Deli Maatschappi N.V.	American Sumatra Tobacco Corp. Bridgeforth Tobacco Co. Kingbridge Tobacco Corp. Viking Drilling Company Triple Five Oil Corp.	Growers and packers of leaf tobacco Petroleum exploration
Koninklyke Industriele Maatschappij Noury & Van der Lande N.V.	Chemetron-Noury Corp. (JV with Chemetron Chemical Corp.)	Peroxide

---

[3] BPM owns 100 per cent of Shell Western Holdings Ltd. which owns 65.3 per cent of Shell Oil. BPM owns an additional 4.1 per cent direct interest in Shell Oil, which, with its subsidiary's interest of 65.3 per cent totals 69.4 per cent, of which 41.6 per cent (60 per cent of the total) is assigned to Royal Dutch Petroleum Co., and 27.8 per cent (40 per cent of the total) is assigned to Shell Transport & Trading Co., Ltd., of England. The same percentages of ownership apply to Shell Chemical Co., which is a division of Shell Oil.

Netherlands (Continued)

Dutch Company

Koninklijke Zwaneberg-Organon N.V. (KZO)	Organon Inc.	Pharmaceuticals
	American Aloe Corp. (53%)	Chemicals, cosmetics
	Cadet Chemical Corp. (50%)	Chemicals
Kuno Van der Horst N.V.	Van der Horst Corp. of America	Electroplating
Maatschappij Van Ber-kel's Patent N.V.	U.S. Slicing Machine Co., Inc.	Scales, measuring instruments
Optische Industrie de Oude Delft N.V.	Aerojet Delft Corp. (JV with Aerojet General Corp.)	Cameras, x-ray image intensifiers, optical equipment
Philips N.V.	U.S. Philips Trust	
Philips Gloeilampen-fabrieken N.V.	North American Philips Inc. (66%)	
Philips Incandescent Lamp Works Holding Co.	Advance Transformer Co.	Transformers
Philips Industries N.V.	AKG Products	Motors
	Alliance Mfg. Co.	Motors, appliances
	Amperex Electronic Corp.	Electron tubes
	Carolina Coach Co.	Bus line
	Chicago Magnet Wire Corp.	Wire
	Dubbings Electronics Inc.	Electronic parts
	Ferroxcube Corp.	Electronic parts
	The A. W. Haydon Co.	Electric timing devices
	Kulka Electric Corp.	Electric components
	Mercury Record Corp.	Recording devices
	Mullard Inc.	Circuitry
	Ohmite Mfg. Co.	Electronic components
	Philips Broadcast Corp.	Audio equipment
	Philips Elmet Corp.	Tungsten, molybdenum
	Plastic-Ware Inc.	Plastic items

Netherlands (Continued)

Dutch Company

	Price Electric Company	Relays and controls
	Pye Communications, Inc.	Communications equipment
	Radiant Lamp Corp.	Radiant lamps
	Science Accessories Corp.	Scientific equipment
	Herman H. Smith Inc.	
	American Aniline Products Inc.	Chemicals and dyestuffs
	Anchor Brush Co., Inc.	Nylon bristle brushes
	Industrial Circuits Co.	Circuitry
	Philips Roxane, Inc.	Biologicals
	Philips Roxane Lab., Inc.	Serums
	Pix Manufacturing	Metal parts and stampings
	Soleau Mfg. Co.	Metal fabrication
	Thompson-Hayward Chemical Company	Agricultural, industrial, and feed chemicals
	Digitronics Corp. (41%)	Data-transmission equipment
	Sessions Clock Co. (81%)	Clocks
	Chappel & Co. (50%)	Music publishing
Royal Dutch Petroleum Co.[4]	Shell Oil Company (41.6%)	Petroleum
	Shell Chemical Co.	Chemicals
Royal Scholten	Morningstar-Paisley Inc.	Flour and adhesive

[4]Royal Dutch Petroleum and Shell Transport & Trading Co., Ltd., of England are holding companies with 60 per cent and 40 per cent interest, respectively, in the Royal Dutch/Shell Group, which consists of Bataafse Petroleum, Shell Petroleum Ltd., and their subsidiaries.

Netherlands (Continued)

Dutch Company

Staatsmijnen (Dutch States Mines)	Columbia Nitrogen Corp.	Nitrogenous fertilizer
	Columbia Nipro Corp. (both Corporations constitute JV's with Pittsburgh Plate Glass. PPG has 51% interest in each.)	Raw material for nylon
Unilever Organization Unilever N.V.[5]	Lever Brothers	Soaps and oils
	T. J. Lipton Co.	Food products
	Good Humor Ice Cream Co.	Frozen dairy products
	Pennsylvania Dutch Megs	Macaroni
	Wishbone Products	Salad dressings
Van Leer Group	Valeron Plastics Inc.	Polyethylene film
Winel Assen	Winel of America Inc.	Tank vent check valves

Netherlands Antilles

Netherlands Antilles Company

Schlumberger Ltd.	Schlumberger Technology Corp.	Electronics
	Western Instrument Inc.	Electronic controls
	Electro-Mechanical Research Inc. (EMR)	Computers, space telemetry
	Heath Co.	Heathkits
	American Systems Inc.	Instrumentations
	Johnston Testers Inc.	Testing equipment
	Dowell Schlumberger Corp. (JV with Dow Chemical)	Well-drilling services
	Solatron Inc.	Test instruments

---

[5] Unilever N.V. and Unilever Ltd., of England are holding companies which constitute the Worldwide Unilever Organization. Although the U.S. firms listed above may be assigned to Unilever N.V., the two parent companies (N.V. and Ltd.) have an agreement providing for an equal distribution of dividends and earnings.

APPENDIX B

Norway

Norwegian Company

Selco A/S	Selco, Inc.	Radomes

Sweden

Swedish Company

Alfa-Laval AB	DeLaval Separator Co. American Heat Reclaiming Co.	Machinery and motor parts
Apotekarnas Kemisku Fabriker Sodertalje AB	Astra Pharmaceutical Products Inc.	Anesthetics
Atvidabergs Industries AB	Facit Inc.	
Barnangens Vademacum	Baranangens Vademacum Inc.	Toothpaste
Ericsson Telefon AB, L. M.	North Electric Co. (31.3%)	Communications equipment
Hoeganaes Gillesholms	Hoganaes Sponge Iron Corp.	Sponge iron, iron powder, and high-alloy powders
Kamyr AB	Kamyr, Inc.	Paper-making equipment
Kockums Mekaniska Verkastads AB	Kockum Industries, Inc. Interconsult Mfg. Co., Inc.	Sawmill equipment Steel pressure tanks
Overman AB	Overman U.S.A. Inc.	Furniture
Pullmax AB	American Pullmax Co.	Shearing machinery
Sandviken Jernverks AB	Sandvik Steel Inc. Sandvik Metals Corp. (JV with United Nuclear Corp.)	Conveyors, springs, tools Zirconium, alloy tubes

Sweden

Swedish Company

Svenska Kullagerfabri-ken AB (Swedish Ball Bearing Co.)	SKF Industries Inc. Tyson Bearing Co. Ried Instrument Co.	Ball and roller bearings Measuring instruments
Svenska Ackumulator Jungner AB	NIFE Inc.	Batteries
Svenska Taendsticks AB (Swedish Match Company)	Transamerican Match Corp.	Matches
Vibro-Verken AB	Vibro Plus Products Inc.	Vibrational construction equipment

Switzerland

Swiss Company

Alusuisse AG	Consolidated Aluminum Corp. Gulf Coast Aluminum Corp.	Aluminum mill and fabrication
CIBA Ltd.	CIBA Agrochemical Co. CIBA Pharmaceutical Co. CIBA Products Company CIBA Chemical & Dye Co. Toms River Chemical Corp. (58%, other 42% owned equally by Geigy and Sandoz)	Agricultural chemicals Pharmaceuticals Epoxy resins Dyes and pigments Chemical plant
Concast AG	Concast Inc. (JV with Mannesmann AG, Germany, and National Steel Corp.)	Installations for continuous casting
Geigy AG, J. R.	Geigy Chemical Corp. Toms River Chemical Corp. (21%)	Chemicals, pharmaceuticals Chemical plant

Switzerland (Continued)

Swiss Company

Heberlein	Heberlein Inc.	Yarn
Hoffman-LaRoche & Co. Ltd.	Hoffman-LaRoche, Inc. Biochemical Procedures Inc.	Pharmaceuticals Medical laboratories
Materiel Industriel SA	Matisa Equipment Corp.	Railroad equipment
Nestle Alimentana SA	Unilac Inc. Nestle Co. Cross & Blackwell Libby, McNeil & Libby (35%) Cain's Coffee	Food products
Oerlikon Machine & Tool Works	Rubber Corporation of America (35%)	Plastic resins
Perrot Dubal Holding SA	Nucon Products Inc.	Scientific equipment
Sandoz Ltd.	Sandoz Inc. Toms River Chemical Corp. (21%)	Pharmaceuticals Chemical plant
Siegfreid AG	Cane's Chemical Works Inc.	Chemicals
Sopinter, SA	Elgin National Watch (I) (25.9%)	Watches, timepieces
Star Unity AG	Star Unity, Inc.	Electric heating units
Suchard AG	Suchard Chocolate Inc.	Food products
Wander AG, Dr. A.	Dorsey Laboratories	Pharmaceuticals

APPENDIX C RECOMMENDATION OF THE
OECD COUNCIL OF MINISTERS
CONCERNING COOPERATION
BETWEEN MEMBER COUNTRIES
ON RESTRICTIVE BUSINESS
PRACTICES AFFECTING
INTERNATIONAL TRADE

(Adopted by the Council at its 149th Meeting on October 5, 1967; the delegate for Switzerland abstained.)

The Council,
HAVING regard to Article 5(b) of the Convention on the Organisation for Economic Cooperation and Development of December 14,1960;

HAVING regard to the Resolution of the Council of December 5, 1961, concerning Action in the Field Restrictive Business Practices and the establishment of a Committee of Experts (OECD, C[61]47, Final);

HAVING regard to the Report by the Committee of Experts on Restrictive Business Practices concerning Cooperation Between Member Countries on Restrictive Business Practices Affecting International Trade (C[67]53);

RECOGNIZING that the diminution of free competition through restrictive business practices may have an adverse effect on achievement of the trade-expansion and economic-growth aims of Member countries as set out in Article 1 of the Convention;

RECOGNIZING that closer cooperation between Member countries is needed in this field but that the present powers of the authorities of Member countries to cooperate are limited to various degrees;

Editor's Note: This document was commented on by J. J. A. Ellis in Chapter 3 and is included here for reference purposes.

RECOGNIZING, moreover, that the unilateral application of national legislation, in cases where business operations in other countries are involved, raises questions as to the respective spheres of sovereignty of the countries concerned;

CONSIDERING therefore that a closer cooperation between Member countries in the form of consultation, exchanges of information, and coordination of efforts on a fully voluntary basis should be encouraged, it being understood that such cooperation should not in any way be construed to affect the legal positions of Member countries with regard to such questions of sovereignty, and in particular the extraterritorial application of laws concerning restrictive business practices, as may arise;

I. RECOMMENDS to the Governments of Member countries:

1.   (a) That insofar as their laws permit, when Member countries undertake under their restrictive business-practices laws an investigation or a proceeding involving important interests of another Member country, they should notify each Member country in a manner and at a time deemed appropriate. Notification should, where appropriate, take place in advance in order to enable the proceeding Member country, while retaining full freedom of ultimate decision, to take account of such views as the other Member country may wish to express and of such remedial action as the other Member country may find it feasible to take under its own laws to deal with the restrictive business practice.

(b) That where two or more Member countries proceed against a restrictive business practice in international trade, they should endeavor to coordinate their action insofar as appropriate and practicable under national laws.

2.   To supply each other with any information on restrictive business practices in international trade which their laws and legitimate interests permit them to disclose.

3.   To cooperate in developing or applying mutually beneficial methods of dealing with restrictive business practices in international trade.

II. INSTRUCTS the Committee of Experts on Restrictive Business Practices to keep under review developments connected with the present Recommendation and to examine periodically the progress made in this field.